Advance Praise for *The Cult of Celebrity*

"Cooper Lawrence's exploration of celebrity culture is one of the most ardent and straightforward analyses that we have. Her expertise on all things celebrity and fame-related makes her the ideal narrator . . . dissecting celebrity involvement in everything from politics and world events to even what kind of lipstick we should buy! All done with her dynamic humor and fervor."

"We love having Cooper contribute to the magazine. She has the rare ability to take what's going on in the celebrity world and break it down in real-life terms. This book explores in depth why 'celebrity' is so important to our culture and why we care, yet it's done with that same genuine, no-pretense style."

—Peter Grossman, *US Weekly Magazine*

"Need a locksmith to the door of understanding? Cooper is a guiding light in a storm, her insight and wisdom light the path to certainty and understanding. Cooper gave me back the power to grow again in this business. Her book The Cult of Celebrity *has that same powerful impact."*

—Christopher Atkins,
Golden Globe–nominated actor; costar, *The Blue Lagoon*

"Cooper Lawrence has keen, compassionate insight into the good, the bad, and the ugly."

—Adrian Zmed, actor, *T. J. Hooker, Grease 2*

"Being with Cooper is like being with one of your closest friends—one who happens to be a treasure trove of humor, wit, ease, incredible sensibility, and a vivacious personality, all wrapped up with intellect and experience."

—Eric Nies, model/actor,
MTV's *Real World* and former host of MTV's *The Grind*

"In a world of lies, deception, ego, and the all-important 'image,' Cooper absolutely helped me keep a clear perception of myself, my goals, and my beliefs. She believed in me and was a strong voice of hope and reason in a time of dire need."

—Jeremy Jackson, actor, *Baywatch*

THE CULT of CELEBRITY

THE CULT of CELEBRITY

What Our Fascination with the Stars Reveals About Us

COOPER LAWRENCE

Foreword by Scott Baio

skirt! is an imprint of The Globe Pequot Press
Guilford, Connecticut

To buy books in quantity for corporate use
or incentives, call **(800) 962–0973**
or e-mail **premiums@GlobePequot.com.**

skirt® is an attitude . . .
spirited, independent, outspoken, serious, playful and irreverent,
sometimes controversial, always passionate.

skirt® is an imprint of The Globe Pequot Press

Design by Sheryl P. Kober

Library of Congress Cataloging-in-Publication Data is available on file.

ISBN: 978-1-59921-335-4

Printed in the United States of America

10 9 8 7 6 5 4 3 2 1

Contents

FOREWORD

Every celebrity has that one moment when they realize they're famous. One actor I know said that his moment came when he went to a Bon Jovi concert, sat in the front row, and not only did the Bon Jovi fans want his autograph but Jon Bon Jovi himself pointed at him from the stage. They may deny it, but fame is a significant and vital part of celebrities' lives, so when it first comes, they savor that moment. Trust me.

The reason some actors thrive while others crash is because they either do or don't recognize the importance of fame. And those who do, crave it. Any actor who tells you that he doesn't want fame is either lying or destined to be a failure. If I said to any potential star, "Take off your clothes and walk down Hollywood Boulevard and you will get a starring role in the next Spielberg movie," they'd be a fool not to do it if they wanted to be famous. Fame brings you power, money, freedom, and security: the power to make choices about your own career; money to not have to take a job you don't want just to pay your bills; the freedom to work when you want to and not work when you don't; and the security that your children will always be cared for. I would like to add one more to this list—existence.

When I was a kid, about 8 or maybe even 10, my father told me a story that I will never forget. My father had just come from the funeral of a man he knew. The funeral for the most part was ordinary except for this: In the midst of the ceremony the son of the deceased man ran to the church windows, flung them open, and began shouting at the top of his lungs, "MY FATHER IS DEAD! . . . MY FATHER IS DEAD!"

I asked my dad, "Why did the son do that?" and he told me, "Because he wanted everyone to know that his father had lived."

It was at that moment that I realized the part of fame and celebrity that has the most meaning for me. It is exactly that. It's proof that I have lived.

If fame is about living, then what happens to an actor who has fame, but loses it? How does that change their view of the life *they* have lived? It's a question that my friends Jason Hervey, Michael Swerdlick,and I had wondered about. Then something amazing happened. Michael had heard a story about a very famous actor who was no longer working in Hollywood, but instead was doing regular blue-collar work. When we heard the name we were floored. He used to be such a star. And then the question changed to "What happens to an actor who had fame and lost it, could he get it back? And more importantly, to what lengths would he go to get it back?"

This idea was crying out to be tested . . . on national television. So we came up with *Confessions of A Teen Idol.* I have a great relationship with VH1 after doing *Scott Baio is 45 and Single* and the subsequent *Scott Baio is 46 and Pregnant* so it was a natural fit. The only piece missing was finding our fame guru, the woman who would turn our idols of the past into celebrities of the present. There was no question in any of our minds: That woman was Cooper Lawrence.

What it means to really have *lived* . . . as a star, and as a celebrity from the perspective of the star makers, the fans, and the stars themselves is revealed in this book. Cooper's unique perspective and unprecedented access exposes certain truths about fame and celebrity that even I didn't realize. Just as there has never been a show about fame rehab, there has never been a book that explains the roots and power of fame and celebrity as clearly as Cooper has . . . and now we have both.

Enjoy.

—Scott Baio

Introduction

When the hit TV show *Scrubs* was shooting its final season with NBC, its star, Zach Braff, posted this on his blog: "The show has been the most fun job I can ever imagine having; going to work everyday and acting like a nerdy goofball with all your friends is a pretty ideal gig for me. Plus now we have an arcade with classic games like 'Paperboy' and 'SpyHunter' just in case the job wasn't sweet enough."

He left out the ridiculous amount of money the cast members were paid to act like "nerdy goofballs" all day together. (According to E! Online, Braff received as much as $350,000 per episode.) No wonder a recent British survey found that kids under ten years old believe the "very best thing in the world" to become is a celebrity. For the 2,500 kids polled, "celebrity" beat out "God," who ranked at only number ten. Clearly He needs a better publicist.

Our fascination with all things celebrity has hit a historic high. Britney Spears claims lead-story status on the AP wire; Paris Hilton going to and from jail is considered breaking news on CNN; and according to the Audit Bureau of Circulations, *People* magazine sells better than *Sports Illustrated, Newsweek,* and *Playboy*.

One of the great American scholars, Charles Eliot Norton, once said, "Such things are never permanent in our country. They burn brightly for a little while, and then burn out." He was referring to the likelihood of the longevity of the *Atlantic,* but he may as well have been referring to celebrity culture. He would have been wrong about both. The *Atlantic,* founded in 1857, is still around today and I suspect now that the genie is out of the bottle, celebrity culture and our attraction to the intricacies of celebrity lives will also endure. But what about more recent additions to our newsstands, celebrity weeklies such as *People, OK!, Us Weekly*? So fast is the turnover of celebrity news that we can barely remember what was in those magazines a month ago—does that mean they will "burn brightly for a little while" and then go up in smoke?

Greta Garbo once said, "If only those who dream about Hollywood knew how difficult it all is." Renowned for living in total seclusion, hidden from the photographers' lenses, she would no doubt be shocked by the media glare that stars now endure 24/7 and by our ravenous appetite for details of even the most intimate aspects of stars' lives. The hounding and sometimes near-total surveillance of celebrities makes the attention stars such as Garbo received look tame.

There was a time not too long ago when gossip and scandal brought the famous down to earth. It humbled them and made them appear more like us, with faults and eccentricities, their lives not so different from ours. That is no longer the case. Today gossip and scandal are the currency of Hollywood: A stint in rehab brings a cache of coolness, a DUI charge translates to extraordinary publicity. Things that were once kept secret—an eating disorder, a childhood of neglect—are revealed on magazine covers and in tell-all books. While this media coverage may give the illusion that stars are just like us, ultimately our attempt to find similarities can only be met with disappointment.

And that's because celebrities hold a unique position in our society. There are only a handful of them, singled out for attention and adoration from their anonymous mass of fans. Their influence is great, and millions of people look to them as experts on everything from fashion to politics. We know their names, every person they've dated, how they decorate their homes, how much they earned last year, the medical crises they've faced, how they lost their baby weight, who they voted for, what toothpaste they use, and just about every other conceivable detail of their lives. Of us, they know . . . nothing.

Actors, singers, and performers struggling to find fame and establish their place in society is not new—but the idea that they are society's elite certainly is. Not so many decades ago, those who we now call celebrities were sometimes even scorned, attacked, or isolated. In his acceptance speech at the Screen Actors Guild (SAG) awards in 2008, actor Javier Bardem said, "My grandparents were actors at a time when actors were not allowed to be buried on sacred land because they were 'homosexuals' and 'prostitutes' so it's been a long way to come here."

In his book *The Frenzy of Renown,* cultural studies expert Leo Braudy notes that it has always been part of the human condition for us to desire fame, but that historically, fame was achieved only by the elite—people such as kings and queens. He suggests that competition arose between the reigning monarchs and artists (such as actors, writers, and painters) over who could best understand and utilize "the new world of media." In the fifteenth century that might have been Gutenberg's printing press, while today it might be the ability to receive news the instant it happens on your cell phone. No matter what the technological advances have been, it seems that the performers and artists are the ones who have been able to capitalize the best, take the crown, and become the new elite.

How did we get to be so celebrity obsessed? More important, what does this obsession mean for our society, our culture, and our daily lives? These are the questions that inspired me to write *The Cult of Celebrity*.

This book is an investigation of why we idolize stars, where their fame comes from, and why we deem them worthy of guiding us through everything from the makeup aisle at Wal-Mart to which candidate or charity to get behind.

I spoke to celebrities themselves. I spoke to entertainment-industry insiders—the media, the producers, the promoters, and the publicists who work in the shadows to help turn ordinary human beings into stars. And I delved into the latest research. The result is a book that explores what makes us so fascinated by celebrities and why we worship them. It explores the narcissism that makes so many people—especially young people—not only want to become celebrities but think they *deserve* to become celebrities. And it looks at how constant media exposure to celebrities affects the way we live our lives today.

Social commentators have begun discussing our fascination with celebrities, and it has influenced the direction of social science research. Many of us find ourselves wondering where the obsession with celebrity came from and what the implications are. These questions need to be answered, as this is about more than idle interest—it's about issues that impact lives. Take one example: The journal *Developmental Psychology* published findings in 2002 that 75 percent of adolescents had a strong attraction to a celebrity and 59 percent were heavily influenced by their favorite star. Great news if their idol is Amy Grant, maybe not so great if it's Amy Winehouse. *The Cult of Celebrity* looks at the facts in order to answer parents' fears that their kids are learning bad habits from their hard-partying starlet idols.

There *are* some positive lessons we can take from celebrities—as long as we are aware of celebrity culture's negative impacts. To that end you'll find plenty of advice from experts so you can take control of the way you and your family consume the celebrity stories you're flooded with every day, and keep them in perspective.

History will remember some of today's stars as great talents who led inspiring lives to be emulated and admired. Others will be reduced to mere Trivial Pursuit questions, if they're lucky. Either way, why do celebrities capture worldwide attention, and what can celebrity culture teach us about ourselves?

Part One

What Is the Cult of Celebrity?

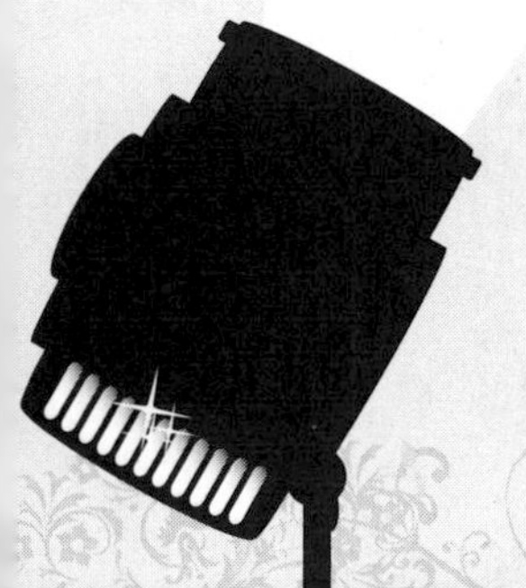

CHAPTER ONE

Worshipping at the Altar of *In Touch Weekly*

Made into heroes and divine beings, stars are not simply objects to be admired; they are objects of worship. Around them the beginnings of a religion are born . . .

EDGAR MORIN, *THE STARS*

When the latest blockbuster movie comes out you know you want to see it if George, Tom, or Brad is in it. When you hear that Britney is at it again, there is no reason to think of anyone other than Britney Spears. Ditto Paris and Lindsay. And you're not going to confuse Beyonce or Oprah with some other Beyonce or Oprah, are you? Those at the very peak of fame need only one name. That's all it takes to identify them from the other six and a half billion or so people on the planet.

Though it may seem like a recent phenomenon, this one-name thing is far from new. It is as old as . . . well, religion. People known by only their first names are just as ubiquitous in the Bible as they are on *Entertainment Tonight*. Moses, Luke, Mary, for starters. I don't need to say "Jesus of Nazareth"—a simple "Jesus" will suffice. "God," too—no explanation necessary.

Okay, so Paris, Britney, and Lindsay might not *quite* be up there with the Holy Trinity—but that doesn't seem to stop us from worshipping them and a multitude of other stars. *People* and *Us*

Weekly sell millions of copies each week. The airwaves are flooded with shows such as *Extra!* and *Access Hollywood* that keep us up-to-date with the minutest details of stars' lives. And who among us has never rushed to tell a friend some juicy celebrity news morsel? Few can resist the attraction of our glamorous twenty-first-century celebrity gods and goddesses.

It has even been shown that the less strict you are about following a religion, the greater the chances are that you will worship celebrities. For decades John Maltby, a renowned psychologist at the University of Leicester in the UK, has been studying the connection between how religious a person is and the degree to which they worship celebrities. Judaism, Christianity, and Islam forbid the worship of all else other than God. But Maltby and his colleagues have found that among religious folk, only the most puritan—those who have a very strong and literal belief in Church authority and divine law—heed this commandment when it comes to celebrity worship. The rest don't see a link between the commandment "Thou shalt worship no other gods" and the time they spend following their favorite celebrities. Or they see the link and simply can't resist the pull of celebrity. Either way, they worship not in the house of the Lord, but at the altar of *In Touch Weekly*. For many of us, celebrity is, in fact, our Church.

One-named Gods and Goddesses

Stars have a magical aura around them—a certain indefinable glowing something that mere mortals don't have. You might call it the "it" factor, or star quality, or charisma—but whatever you call it, there is no denying that stars are set apart from the rest of us. We perform rituals in our spare time to show our devotion to them:

We read magazines, watch certain shows, discuss them, and in the case of true fans, collect autographs and memorabilia—to make a kind of shrine, if you will.

But does all of that really mean celebrities have been elevated to the status of gods and goddesses in our society? I'm the first to admit I am no scripture scholar, but even so, I can't help seeing a few similarities . . .

All-seeing, All-knowing, All-powerful

Let's start with an important requirement: A deity has to be present everywhere, all around us, at all times. Unless you're reading this book while orbiting Earth on the International Space Station, it should be pretty apparent to you that celebrities pass this test. Though a star may be quickly replaced by the next "it" person who warrants having only one name, when he or she is at the height of fame, his or her every move is on our radar. Some celebrities remain in our consciousness for generations (Marilyn Monroe is a good example), while some have all the staying power of a firefly (remember Sanjaya?), but the need for *celebrity itself* endures. Celebrity has soaked into every part of our culture: Everywhere you turn you find the faces of celebrities looking at you.

Celebrity has soaked into every part of our culture.

If I remember correctly, a divine being must also be all-powerful. According to a July 2007 article in London's *Daily Star*, Madonna has the power to command that her dressing room be supplied with 144 boxes of strawberries, Yorkshire tea, a skipping rope, organic green tea, vanilla room spray, and eight full-length mirrors. The Smoking Gun, a Web site owned by Court TV, published a 2000 tour rider showing that Christina Aguilera demanded a police escort on the way to her shows because "under no circumstances" is she to "be allowed to encounter any delays due to traffic." In an amazing (and much more humanitarian) example of celebrity clout, in 2006 George Clooney was given the opportunity to address the United Nations' Security Council about the Darfur crisis.

The latter is a good example of how celebrities' power and influence spreads beyond their field of expertise. At the selfless end of the scale we have stars influencing world leaders and the public on the environment, politics, world debt, and world peace. And at the more self-serving end of the scale, we have stars creating their own mini-empires. Singers become actors, and vice versa. Then they become successful fashion designers. They start their own movie, TV, or recording companies. Or they launch perfume, jewelry, watch, makeup, or handbag lines.

A god or goddess must also be all knowing. I'm certainly not about to suggest that our favorite celebrities know the meaning of life or have all the answers—but it doesn't stop them from volunteering their opinions on every conceivable topic. And the media and fans can't get enough of it. Celebrities are constantly being quoted on subjects that have nothing to do with their skill or talent. You probably don't know what acting techniques Tom has studied—but you know what he thinks about psychiatry. It's doubtful you know what vocal exercises Madonna practices—but I bet you know an awful lot more about Kabbalah since she became an adherent. From relationships to evening-gown designers, from parenting to the best type of yoga—celebrities are portrayed as having knowledge about all aspects of life.

Their perspective on news events even seems more noteworthy than ordinary people's. When Suzanne Somers lost her Malibu house to a fire in January 2007, she got to go on Larry King to discuss it, despite the fact that several other homes were lost as well. Where was those poor schnooks' chance to garner our sympathies? (Okay, okay, rich schnooks—it is Malibu, after all; I don't think they have poor people there. But you get my point.)

Up on a Pedestal

Any self-respecting god or goddess also needs to be superior to ordinary folk; he or she has to seem special. And from down here in everyday land, few beings in this world appear more special than celebrities. They seem to have more of everything—everything you want or aspire to, or fantasize about having, that is. They have more beauty, more talent, more confidence . . . more wealth, cars, homes, diamonds, boats, and planes . . . more adoration and appreciation. They also have more freedom and flexibility in their careers and lifestyle choices, and more opportunities to express themselves. They enjoy more excitement in their lives, and more options. When their first marriage breaks down, they don't turn to match.com or their aunt who said she'd fix them up with a blind date. No, they choose from an array of celebrity entertainers, sports stars, businesspeople, or models, and they have their "people" arrange the meeting. When they get a few friends together for a party, the guest list reads like the nominations for the Oscars and the Grammys combined. Everything they do just appears to be more fun and more glamorous than ordinary life.

There is no denying that on top of what celebrities have already earned, people are constantly giving them extras that you and I don't receive. They get better service in restaurants and hotels and better seats at shows and movies. They receive gift bags of luxury products, even though they could afford to buy them many times over. According to a 2005 article in *USA Today,* some companies had advertising divisions that catered solely to ensuring their gifts ended up in celebrities' hands, with the aim that celebrities would be photographed using their products. For many years celebrity SWAG (stands for "stuff we all get") was literally a free-for-all, but in January 2007 the IRS stepped in, reminding the stars that any promotional gifts they receive need to be declared as taxable income. As a result the celebrity gift basket has been downsized, but at its peak, a typical gift basket for the Oscars could be worth upward of $100,000. *Access Hollywood* reported that for the 2007 Golden Globes the gift bag, worth over $20,000, consisted of "a $2,000 gym membership, a $1,200 diamond pendant, an $865 Chopard watch and a $475 camera phone, plus handbags, MP3 players and a slew of gift certificates."

At its peak, a typical gift basket for the Oscars could be worth upwards of $100,000.

Although the stars may be receiving less swag these days, they still get past velvet ropes into exclusive clubs—even if they are underage. (In 2006 it didn't occur to anyone to check Lindsay Lohan's ID, apparently.) And in situations where any one of us regular people would have immediately been thrown in the slammer, celebrities manage to continually postpone their court dates, à la Nicole Richie and her DUI charge; or they get let out of jail early, as in the case of Paris Hilton after her conviction for driving on a suspended license. Granted, for Paris the whole debacle didn't work out so well in the end—but still, if it had been you suffering from claustrophobia in that cell, I very much doubt the authorities would've sent you home for hair extensions and your favorite cupcakes, even if it was just for a day or so.

We have no way of knowing whether celebrities' lives are really as peachy as they seem. Like the rest of us, they probably have good days and bad days, concerns and anxieties. There is, however, one desirable thing that we have a whole lot more of than celebrities do: privacy. And if the media coverage is any indication, there is one thing they seem to have a lot more of that we *don't* want: substance abuse problems.

Even if our perception of stars as being better than us and having more of the good things in life is partly fantasy, this only heightens celebrities' mystique and pushes their pedestal higher and higher into the clouds. And after all, perceptions are everything in celebland.

Perfect Goodness

Fans treat celebrities like gods and goddesses in another important way: by considering them to be fundamentally perfect and good, regardless of what they do. True fans explain away the indiscretions of their favorite stars, no matter how reprehensible or "in your face" they may be. This can be anything from Mel Gibson fans continuing to be devoted to him even after his disturbing drunken anti-Semitic tirade, to those who forgave Hugh Grant his dalliances with a certain lady of the evening. Fans still fork over hard-earned cash to see their movies, and spend valuable time reading in-depth articles about them or watching interviews on late-night talk shows.

We do not afford ordinary people the same adulation and unconditional forgiveness. When O. J. Simpson was on trial for murdering his wife, the nation was divided. For all who assumed his guilt, there were as many people ready to spring to his defense. But when Scott Peterson faced charges for murdering his wife and unborn baby, everyone immediately assumed he was guilty, even before the trial began. If Julia Roberts had been the runaway bride in real life instead of Jennifer Wilbanks of Duluth, Georgia, we would have said, "Oh, she's under so much pressure with the films and the paparazzi following her; we understand poor Julia."

If misbehavior won't make us reject our favorite stars, it's no wonder that when they do something *good* they seem almost superhuman. One day during a CNN report on the latest deadly weapon being used against our troops in Iraq, across the crawl came a story about George Clooney paying $20 for a cup of lemonade to a group of children who had set up a stand near where he was filming *Leatherheads*. You can just picture the production intern saying to the group of young entrepreneurs, "This is from George, he said to keep the change," and it was newsworthy.

Sometimes it really *is* newsworthy. There was that story all over the media years ago about Tom Cruise encountering a hit-and-run accident victim while driving through Santa Monica. Not only did he stay with her until help arrived, he paid her $7,000 medical bill when he found out she was uninsured. And he didn't stop there. At the London premiere of *Mission Impossible,* Cruise saw two boys being crushed by the crowd of 10,000 and pulled them to safety. Later one of the boys said, "He's my hero."

The Cult of *Star Trek*

Here's something interesting: There has actually been research done about *Star Trek* fans and how some of them view *Star Trek* as a religion. In and of itself, this phenomenon could fill a book, but suffice to say, trekkies perform many religious acts and practices that are often associated with conventional religions.

In *Star Trek,* Gene Roddenberry created a utopia, an ideal world that when the series was first shown on TV in 1966 did not reflect the real state of the country. The crew of the starship *Enterprise* was made up of a mix of races and genders, and all were considered equals, at a time when not all races and genders were considered equal in real-life society.

In 2001, marketing academic Robert Kozinets explained *Star Trek* as "a utopian refuge for the alienated and disenfranchised." Like religion, *Star Trek* becomes a larger social identity for these fans, just as being Jewish or Catholic might. This explains why it has attracted so many lost souls, again as religion sometimes does.

Make fun of the *Star Trek* geek at your peril, as they are some of the most intelligent and imaginative of enthusiasts. In his book *Textual Poachers: Television Fans and Participatory Culture,* Henry Jenkins applauds the fertile minds of *Star Trek* fans who suggest scripts and alternative plot lines for their favorite characters to follow, in the most creative and respectful of ways.

Why Do People Celebrity Worship?

It's tempting to think that celebrities have some inherent quality or special power that makes people worship and adore them. The name sometimes given to that notion is charisma. Max Weber, one of the founders of modern sociology, defined *charisma* as "a certain quality of an individual personality by virtue of which he is considered extraordinary and treated as endowed with supernatural, superhuman or at least specifically exceptional powers or qualities." Celebrities have that.

> "There are just people who will always be famous no matter how much or how little they promote themselves. There's just something about them."
>
> —JARETT WEISELMAN

Former senior editor for *In Touch Weekly* magazine Jarett Weiselman says that in the time he has been writing about and observing celebrity behavior, "There are just people who will always be famous no matter how much or how little they promote themselves. There's just something about them that is so intriguing, innate, and original. We will be drawn to them no mater what. Madonna, for example—she has that 'it' factor and the minute you first saw her you knew, and it is still true today."

So, can the explosion in our celebrity worshipping in the past few decades be the result of simply an excess of charismatic individuals? I think it's highly unlikely, when you consider that celebrities can now be hatched from lives in which any exceptional powers or qualities were seemingly nonexistent—think Paris Hilton and Nicole Richie. Reality TV stars are another good example: Reality TV has perhaps shown that the kind of charismatic aura Weber describes isn't necessarily inherent in stars, but is something that we can gradually come to see in them.

Are celebrities smarter than we are; is that how they have found a way into our psyche and our personal thoughts? According to Jay Zagorsky, a research scientist at Ohio State University, that is highly unlikely as well. His research published in 2007 in the journal *Intelligence* finds that people with below-average IQ scores are just as successful as people with above-average IQ scores.

We may never fully solve the riddle of what makes human beings worship celebrities. But as we've already seen, our attitude toward religion is known to have some influence. And one other thing researchers have been able to establish is that our personalities play a big part too.

Celebrity Worshippers: Who Are You?

For most of us, celebrity worship is all about fun and entertainment. We do it for *social reasons*—because we enjoy talking to our friends about the latest news on, say, Johnny Depp or Brad Pitt. If this is why you like to follow the lives of celebrities, science shows that you probably have an extravert personality, which means you tend to be outgoing and like to engage with your environment and the people around you.

A smaller percentage of celebrity worshippers are motivated by the belief that they have an *intense connection* with their favorite celebrity. They believe that if they met their favorite celebrity, the star would understand them and perhaps be their friend, or that their favorite celebrity is truly their soul mate. To get an idea of this type of celebrity worshipper, think of the film *Notting Hill.* When Anna, a famous Hollywood actress (played by Julia Roberts), and Honey, the sister of Anna's new paramour (Hugh Grant), meet for the first time, Honey gushes about how much she adores the actress and how beautiful she is and says, "I genuinely believe and have believed for some time now that we can be best friends."

According to studies, this type of celebrity worshipper tends to be higher in the trait *neuroticism.* These are the worriers of the world—those who tend to be nervous, a bit on the high-strung side, and possibly insecure.

Researchers such as John Maltby have also found that celebrity worshippers are more likely to suffer from *narcissism,* a personality disorder characterized by a grandiose sense of self, an inflated sense of superiority over others, a lack of empathy, and an excessive need to be admired. You may have heard the phrase "sense of entitlement"—well, yes, that too is one of the characteristics of a narcissistic personality. It may sound counterintuitive that someone so into themselves, who cares very little about others, would worship celebrities, but according to researchers Diane Ashe, John Maltby, and Lynn E. McCutcheon, narcissists oscillate between feeling disdain for others and over-idealizing them, which is easy to do with a celebrity. And narcissists like to be domineering in all social situations. So for a narcissist is there any better role model than a scene-stealing celebrity?

There is one more psychological factor to consider: A person's view on how fair the world is. In psychology there is a theory—the *Just World Theory*—that deals with how strongly a person believes the world is a fair and *just* place, and that bad people get punished and good people get rewarded. A person may fall at either the believing or disbelieving end, or anywhere along the spectrum. Researcher McCutcheon was interested in the Just World Theory and how it relates to celebrity worship. What he found was that those who believe strongly that the world is a just place are likely to be avid celebrity worshippers. In a 2003 issue of *Current Research in Social Psychology* he said, "Someone who believes that the *world* is 'just' is likely to believe that the major components of society are fair, and the *celebrity* system is a major component of contemporary society."

For a narcissist is there any better role model than a scene-stealing celebrity?

Challenging the Cult of Celebrity

There are several theories for why so many stars go by one name—Madonna, Cher, Fergie, Rihanna, and so on. Some have said that publicists and handlers intentionally use one name as a way to

The Holy Toast

I really got a sense of the intense connection that some fans feel toward their favorite celebrities when I was filling in at radio station Z100 in New York and Justin Timberlake had left a half-eaten piece of French toast behind. It was March 2000, and Justin had come in with the rest of 'N Sync to have breakfast and chat on air. Folks at the station decided it would be funny to put the remnants of Justin's French toast and the fork he'd used on eBay.

Not only did the eBay auction make national news, but the French toast sold for over $3,000 (the proceeds were donated to charity). I had to wonder about that Timberlake fan who handed over hard-earned cash for an old, half-eaten breakfast.

True religion wins out here, though. In 2004 a ten-year-old grilled cheese sandwich that was said to bear the image of the Virgin Mary went for $28,000 on eBay. Of course I can't speculate on how much it would've sold for if it had been Justin's image on the grilled cheese sandwich—but I'm pretty sure that the big money would be on an image of the Virgin Mary appearing on Justin Timberlake.

make the celebrity seem so famous he or she only needs one name to be recognized. Using only one name adds to the iconic nature of the celebrity and is designed to make him or her seem otherworldly, above us in a stratosphere that we—mere mortals—will never attain.

Jarett Weiselman has an opposing theory. "Referring to a celebrity by one name actually speaks to how familiar we feel with that celebrity. I don't refer to my friend as 'Jody Miller,' I call her 'Jody.' We don't use last names with people we are comfortable with, or with people we know well, and I think that's what certain celebrities—Paris, Lindsay, and Britney in particular—are really good at," he says.

"If I said 'Natalie,' you would say, 'Natalie Imbruglia? Natalie Merchant? Natalie Portman?' You wouldn't be sure which Natalie I meant, and that is because those women keep their lives private—but those particular girls who are known by one name let the world into their lives in such an unbelievable way, [the use of only one name] makes sense. They are your friends and you know a lot about them."

Jeannine Hill Fletcher, Th.D., professor of theology at Fordham University, thinks there is a common root to the adoption of a single name in both celebrity worship and religious worship, but she points to a crucial difference: "One offers something surface while the other offers something lasting." Fletcher cautions that celebrity worshippers need to be able to recognize what is really lasting and what it is about a celebrity's life that they admire. "The celebrity and your familiarity with them is not enough. What about their life matters to you, and what images are you being offered that have real staying power for you?" she says. "The lives of the holy ones are lives whose persuasiveness survives. There is a reason that after 2,000 years

Jesus, Buddha, and Mohammed still endure." Regarding celebrities, she asks, "Are these lives that last?"

Philosopher John Hick says that what all religious traditions have in common is that they offer us a way to turn away from our self-centeredness to turn to God, or other-centeredness, and lead lives that are more authentic and full—while celebrity worship *encourages* us to be self-centered. Do we really need help being any more self-centered than we already are? Media images have the power to shape us, as do religious figures. The question is: How do we want to be shaped?

Ask yourself what your ultimate concern is. Is it fame? Popularity? Or is it something deeper and longer lasting?

Fletcher believes that everyone, whether religious or not, has an ultimate concern that drives his or her life. Ask yourself what your ultimate concern is. Is it fame? Popularity? Or is it something deeper and longer lasting?

There are other examples to follow than celebrities, she reminds us: "The lives of the saints in the various holy traditions emphasize the character of their lives. We understand that they too did bad things, but the religious narrative is that the [good] qualities do overcome, as part of the human condition." She believes their stories show us that we too can "transform ourselves to become those persons that we want to be."

Celebrity—A Long Tradition

The concept of celebrity is not new. The majority has long had an insatiable interest in the lives of the privileged few. Kings and queens, gladiators and army commanders, Olympic athletes (as in the original Greek Olympics, 776 B.C., not Michelle Kwan and Dara Torres)—those were the stars of their day.

Let me walk you through a historical example of celebrity life, from Spain, circa the early 1500s. A very prominent family had a handsome son with a taste for all the temptations that fame and money offered, especially the ladies. He was a renowned playboy and addicted to gambling. He was also not above engaging in swordplay—and everyone knew it. (In the modern era, this is similar to scandalous photos of a celeb holding a gun or knife surfacing on the Internet.) One night he, his brother, and some other relatives ambushed members of a rival family. When word got out, he had to run and hide—sort of a 1500s equivalent to racing off to rehab. Like many in prominent positions today, he used his family name and his celebrity to get him out of trouble, and he avoided prosecution.

However, unlike celebrities of today who are happy with their "get out of jail free" card, this young man was transformed by spiritual teachings. He spent time studying the scriptures, renounced his old life, and became a saint. Literally.

This is the story of St. Ignatius Loyola, the founder of the Jesuits. From playboy to saint . . . it would make a great *E! True Hollywood Story,* don't you think?

CHAPTER TWO

Love, Hate, Awe— Our Perplexing Relationship with the Stars

They can't let go for the same reasons that we can't let go. We're engaged in a mutually destructive relationship with the world's unstable citizens.

HEATHER HAVRILESKY, TV CRITIC, SALON.COM

On my radio show we do a daily segment called "News from the Corner," which is made up of one serious news story (human interest mostly, like which city has the worst traffic and other stuff that makes you say, "Huh, that's interesting"), two celebrity stories, and two offbeat news stories.

Much like the rule of etiquette that one must not discuss politics or religion at the dinner table, I have a rule for this segment, which in fact applies to my whole show: Ridicule or harsh words are forbidden when discussing Tori Spelling, or as I call her, "*my* Tori." I love her so much that I was about to fly out to her Studio City, California, home when she had her public yard sale—until I learned that she doesn't wear a size 7 shoe (my size) and I figured, "What's the point, it was her shoe collection I was after. "

One time on my show, actor Zachary Quinto came on to discuss his television series *Heroes,* but all I wanted to know about was Tori, since he played her best friend on her sitcom, *So noTO-RIous*. I love Tori like a gay man loves . . . well, Tori, I suppose. I have never met her, never will, and I suspect that in real life she would not be seen with the likes of me—yet I defend her to the death. You are not allowed to say anything negative about *my* Tori. You can imagine how thrilled I was when Tori let us into her life with her first reality show *Tori & Dean Inn Love* and her subsequent *Tori & Dean: Home Sweet Hollywood.* Now I know private details that I may have missed otherwise.

You probably know more intimate details of some celebrities' lives than of the colleagues you sit next to at work every day. You might know the latest on everything in a star's life (whom they're dating this month, where they went for their vacation, how much they paid for their house, how many grams of carbs they eat a day) but have trouble remembering your best friend's birthday or how old your niece is so you don't buy her a Barbie doll for Christmas when she comes to visit with her husband. You might know more of a celebrity's closely guarded secrets and inner feelings than of your own teenage son or daughter. And this is a person who has no idea that you even exist.

Most other relationships in your life are a two-way street. You can talk freely to the other person and ask questions; the two of you respond to each other, exchange your opinions and news; you can read each other's facial expressions and gauge each other's tone of voice. Celebrities, on the other hand, are the ones doing all the talking. They speak to you from the movie screen, the TV, the radio, or the pages of a magazine. Sometimes it even seems as if they are talking directly to *you*—when they happen to sing, play a role, or say something that strikes a chord with you. But the communication is all one-way. Of course, you could always talk back to the TV, the radio, or your iPod, but if you receive an answer, you probably need something a little stronger than this book to help you.

The number of people we know in the "artificial world"—actors, singers, sportspeople, TV hosts—is much larger than the number of people we know in the real world.

The Illusion of Intimacy

Researchers have a few fancy-pants terms for the puzzling relationship we have with celebrities, but perhaps the best one is also the oldest. Back in the 1950s, when television was taking off in a big way and bringing celebrities into lounge rooms all across the country, two researchers (Donald Horton and R. Richard Wohl) became intrigued by the one-sided relationship between a viewer and the celebrity on the screen. In a 1956 article in the journal *Psychiatry*, they argued that it all came down to "the illusion of intimacy." We have a seemingly intimate relationship with celebrities: We become very familiar with them because they're continually looking out at us from a screen or the pages of a magazine. Let's be honest here, we probably see their faces as often as we see some of our friends'. And we know an extraordinary amount of personal information about them.

The intimacy is all an illusion, though, because these celebrities don't know us from Eve. The truth is, if we see Nicole Kidman on the street, no matter how big a fan we are or how much we've read about her, she still won't have any idea who we are.

In the 1970s, University of Maryland researcher J.L. Caughey coined the term *artificial social relations*, and in an article that appeared in *American Quarterly* suggested that the number of people we know in the "artificial world"—actors, singers, sportspeople, TV hosts—is much larger than the number of people we know in the *real* world.

And it makes us want to get closer and closer to these people. As we become caught up in a song we love, or the storyline of an addictive TV show, we inevitably find ourselves wanting to know more about the real people behind them. According to a 2006 report titled "State of the News Media" published by Journalism .org, in the early 2000s sales of major news magazines such as *Time* and *Newsweek* went down noticeably. Meanwhile sales of entertainment magazines such as *People* and *Us Weekly* skyrocketed, even though they faced increased competition from a slew of new celebrity-watching mags that came on the market. Meanwhile, celebrity "news" shows on TV multiplied at a rapid rate. There's a craving for knowledge about stars' personal lives that can never quite be satisfied, because the feeling of *real* closeness will always elude us. It's no wonder these magazines and TV shows are such big business. And it's more than just commerce; our relationship with the stars may affect us personally.

That we get caught up in these illusory relationships with celebrities may have a lot to do with difficulties in our real relationships. According to a 2004 study published in the *North American Journal of Psychology*, people tend to turn to celebrities to satisfy needs that are not being met in conventional ways. For instance, if you find your real relationships too complex and difficult to manage, you might be happy with a one-sided relationship with a celebrity. The ease of that relationship and the lack of challenge might be a welcome relief. Similarly, if you tend to be shy, you might take comfort in your connection with a celebrity—a connection that does not require you to engage socially. You don't have to shower and do your hair, or get anxious about thinking of something to add to a conversation, if you're watching a Matt Damon movie on your couch while flicking through the latest issue of *Star* magazine.

People who feel their lives are void of interesting experiences may follow the lives of celebrities as a way to vicariously enjoy a more exciting lifestyle. Vicarious enjoyment is one reason we watch movies and TV shows in the first place—for the vivid feelings that we experience about a fictional world. When the son doesn't come back from battle, we feel real loss; we may even shed a tear while sitting there staring at the screen. Or when, at the end of a romance, the heroine finds that he *does* love her—and always did—we are overjoyed. Same goes for the relationship we might develop with celebrities while following their lives in the pages of a magazine: Feeling their highs (career success, marriage, pregnancy) and their lows (box-office flop, divorce, fertility issues).

Jarett Weiselman says, "The reason people open celebrity weeklies is to live vicariously through these celebrities: To wear what they wear; to go to the clubs that they go to; and to roll in the circles that they roll in. It's escapism; it's complete vicarious living."

Our Friends on the Small Screen

When it comes to TV stars, our relationships with them can get complicated, because we might feel an illusory intimacy with not only a star but with his or her character, too. This is especially true for actors in long-running soaps or shows that are on endless reruns, such as that perennial favorite, *Friends.* The characters of these shows, and the actors who play them, become incredibly familiar, because they are with us all the time, like family members. Jennifer Aniston has said that when *Friends* was a prime-time show, people would approach her on the street and yell at her for something disagreeable her character, Rachel Green, did.

Leven Rambin knows this experience all too well. She stars as two characters—Lily Montgomery and her half-sister Ava Benton—in the daytime drama *All My Children.* She is used to fans merging her and her characters' identities and calling her by her characters' names. She says, "These characters are in your life every single day if you are a soap opera fan, so [the actors] *are* those people."

Rick Hearst, who plays villain Ric Lansing on *General Hospital,* spent the best part of an online chat session with fans on the Web site SOAPnet trying to establish that he is *not* the character and that the writer controls his character. (Lansing is notorious for kidnapping, adultery, deception—oh, and for sleeping with his stepdaughter—so I guess it's no wonder Hearst was keen to claim his own identity.) Fans kept asking him to defend or justify his character's bad-boy antics, and he responded by saying things such as, "I guess you'd have to ask the writers!" or "People seem to think that I'm in charge of the destiny of this character." Eventually he simply entreated the fans to make their displeasure with his character known to the writers so that they might give Lansing a chance at redemption. "I throw my hands out to all of my fans. I implore them to write in and say what you feel about this character," Hearst said.

Stephen Collins played Reverend Eric Camden on the longest-running TV family drama *7th Heaven*, and it seems that being mistaken for a man of the cloth might be a little easier to deal with. Collins told me, "The longer the show was on, the more people tended to treat me as if I really were a minister. This has made it easier to be gracious to people who stop me in public or who might seek me out to get an autograph."

"I'm grateful for fans. Without them, we [actors] have no careers."

—STEPHEN COLLINS

On the whole it doesn't trouble him that fans feel a powerful connection to him/Reverend Camden and approach him in public to talk, even though he doesn't know them. But he does try to put a polite distance between himself and a fan, especially when he's out with his family. "You don't usually engage in long conversations or give people a phone number or address, and 99.99% of the time they don't expect it," he says. "I'm grateful for fans. Without them, we [actors] have no careers."

On rare occasions Collins has crossed the barrier between himself and a fan, turning an illusory relationship into a real one.

He struck up a lasting friendship with a child therapist in Iowa who wrote to tell him she was using an earlier role he played, in a series called *Tales of the Gold Monkey,* as part of her therapy for a boy who had been beaten by his father and uncle and was terrified of adult males. "The therapist had seen my show and noticed instinctively that my character was both physically strong *and* gentle. This combination of traits turned out to be a revelation to the child, and the therapist helped the boy fashion an imaginary relationship with my TV character. It helped the kid to slowly work back some trust with men," Collins said. He went on to correspond for years through the therapist with another child undergoing therapy, and even flew to Iowa to attend the boy's high school graduation. "I've never regretted it," he said.

When Worlds Collide

So what is it like for us regular folk to come face-to-face with our idols? There are two kinds of celebrity encounters: the lucky coincidences that result in a star sighting and the planned events where star-struck fans line up for hours for just two seconds with their favorite celeb. Each kind of encounter can have a potentially long-lasting impact on fans.

The Chance Celebrity Encounter

For most of us in a faux-intimate relationship with a favorite star, the best we can hope for is that truly shocking and amazing occurrence: the chance celebrity meeting, when a star's world collides with ours and suddenly, unexpectedly, we're sharing the same public space.

If this has ever happened to you, perhaps you felt special and blessed—perhaps even as though some of the star's aura was wearing off on you. You might have called out his or her name

Too Much Intimacy?

Sometimes the illusion of intimacy seems to work against a celebrity. Becoming so familiar with a celebrity, seeing his or her face everywhere we turn, and learning too many details about his or her private life, can color our perception of them. Take Angelina Jolie. Critics praised her performance in *A Mighty Heart* and said that it was the best of her career up to that point. But even as they were predicting another Oscar coming her way, the film was crashing and burning at the box office. Did moviegoers know too much about Jolie as a person to enjoy her in that role? Did they fail to take her seriously because of all the footage of her and Brad Pitt and the odd stories surrounding them? Some Hollywood observers blamed the box office disappointment on what has been termed *Brangelina fatigue.* Perhaps seeing a celebrity's face everywhere sometimes makes us want to see them nowhere.

excitedly as you rummaged around in your handbag looking for something he or she could sign—a trophy.

Or you might have simply sat there, frozen with awe, as a friend of mine did at Starbucks one morning when he was sitting enjoying a latte and in walked his greatest boyhood crush, Molly Ringwald. Now, I'm not talking just any early teen crush. He had compulsively written her letters, and in his lofty position as editor, had virtually turned his school newspaper into *The World According to Molly Ringwald.* Even in his thirties, he still has an ancient *Pretty in Pink* video he refuses to part with. In Starbucks that morning his wife couldn't understand why he'd stopped responding to her as she tried to discuss something in the paper. Then she looked up and saw his pale, stricken face and thought, "Oh my God, I've got to call 911." Turned out Molly had been at the counter for a few minutes, but he had been unable to say or do anything. She slipped straight past them and out the door into a waiting limo with her iced mocha before he even had a chance to regain full consciousness, let alone ask for an autograph.

Star sightings can have this kind of effect on us ordinary human beings. There is a touch of the religious experience to it and the shock of reality meeting fantasy. It's as if we're going about our business when all of a sudden this being steps out of the screen or off the page of a magazine into our everyday lives. And there's a hint of the mythical in it as well. Even though we know celebrities are human beings, in our minds they also exist on some higher plane, out of reach.

Let's break the whole celebrity-sighting thing down and look at why it has this effect on people. Say you happen to be visiting New York City with a girlfriend and you go eat at a deli. You're about to sink your teeth into a delicious-looking Reuben sandwich when you notice something out of the corner of your eye: a swish of blonde hair, a familiar face. Your brain registers: "Who do I know in New York?" You turn to look properly, and it takes you a couple of seconds to realize it's in fact Sarah Jessica Parker and Matthew Broderick having pastrami on rye two tables away.

You kick your friend under the table and whisper to her who it is. While your friend takes out her cell phone and tries to look like she's casually making a call (though she's taking a snapshot of the celebrity couple), you phone your friends back home to say, "Hey, guess who is eating a few tables away from us?!" All the while, you're taking what you hope are subtle glances at the pair, cataloging important details you have to remember for the stories you'll tell later: What they're wearing and eating; whether they're polite to the waiter; how loving they're acting toward each other and their son, James; how well behaved James is; and so on.

It's given you a thrill, it's made your trip to New York more memorable, and you feel kinda special. You just *know* that your friends back home—with whom you discussed every nuance of *Sex and the City* as intensely as a book club discusses the latest Oprah pick—are going to be steamed they didn't come on vacation with you.

Now let's say Sarah Jessica gets up and walks over to ask if she can borrow the spicy mustard off your table. Dumbfounded, you hand her the mustard, unable to speak because you weren't expecting to actually interact with this celebrity. Then she says, "Thanks. You can't have a pastrami sandwich without the spicy mustard, right?"

"I've never tried spicy mustard," you manage to say.

And the celebrity says, with her winning smile, "Really, you should, it's New York 101." And off she goes to her lucky sandwich at her lucky table with her famous husband and their adorable child. This has taken things to the next level: You've gone from celebrity sighting to celebrity *encounter.* If Sarah Jessica sees you the next day, she might recognize *you.*

A celebrity encounter really rocks our world because celebrities' lives seem greater than ours. Theirs is an existence of remarkable occurrences and lucky tables, wonderful husbands, and perfect offspring. Most people idealize what a celebrity must be like in person, which is why it is so startling when he or she steps out of that idealized realm for a moment and enters our own ordinary existence. For a moment, the celebrity's universe is our universe; her bottle of spicy mustard is our bottle of spicy mustard. Our mundane life has intersected with the glamorous and exotic. We matter now on a whole new level, and will be able to tell this story at parties forever . . . or at least until the celebrity stops being famous. But now we have something very special that makes the celebrity encounter even juicer, and that is *exclusive* information: Something we alone know or experienced with this celebrity. This exclusivity makes the occurrence all the more sweet and us all the more entertaining when we recount the story later on, especially if what the star did is something mundane our listeners can relate to.

Magazines that publish photos of celebrities doing everyday things are operating on this very principle. It's news when a celebrity pushes a grocery cart in Brentwood, grabs a shake at Baja Fresh, walks their dog in Beverly Hills . . . or passes gas in public. Case in point: I was living in New York when Woody Harrelson was filming one of his movies. Harrelson, a renowned yoga enthusiast, and his yoga instructor began coming to my gym to do their yoga. They were kind enough to allow the rest of us into their class, and we downward-dogged right alongside the movie star. One day in class, my mat was situated behind the *Cheers* star when all of a sudden—*poot!*— Harrelson let rip a mighty wind. He was such a lovely man, I felt terrible gossiping about it, but how could I resist? It was news; and the headline reads "Woody Harrelson is human and does stuff that humans do, like pass gas." C'mon, admit it, you enjoyed finding out that little tidbit, didn't you? That's because it is exclusive information that only I knew—and now you know.

One theory suggests that celebrity sightings and encounters are exciting for the same reason that overhearing or spying something gossipworthy in everyday life is exciting. Research published in the journal the *Psychological Record* in 2006 says that what we really enjoy about gossip is the entertainment factor we provide to others in the telling of it. It actually enhances our social relationship with our friends and family. Similarly, if we entertain our friends and family by sharing a story of a celebrity experience, we improve our social bond. It brings us closer together.

My grandfather used to talk about the time he met Albert Einstein at a party as if it were happening to him over and over again.

Another explanation comes from *Social Identity Theory*, developed by social psychologists Henri Tajfel and John C. Turner to explain why we favor some folks over others. We each feel better about who we are and our own identity when we belong to a group, especially one that we deem superior to other groups. When you or someone in your social circle—known as your *in-group*—shares news of a celebrity sighting or encounter, it suddenly expands your in-group to include a celebrity. Your social identity is now one of someone who, in a sense, knows a person with a privileged and superior status in society.

The thrill of bumping into a celebrity can also be explained by something social psychologists call *BIRGing*, which stands for "basking in reflected glory." This happens in everyday life, too.

For instance, say your sister wins a book award. You might find that you take a vicarious pride in her accomplishments, and you start telling everyone in your social circle about her award so that they can congratulate you for having such an impressive sister. (This is similar to when siblings of celebrities garner attention despite their lack of talent or lack of desire to be in the industry.)

In the situation of the celebrity encounter, we may feel as if some part of the celebrity has rubbed off on us—the air he or she breathes or his or her energy, charisma, or in the case of the time I interviewed Renée Zellweger and she accidentally sprayed a tiny bit of spit on me, saliva. When we have a celebrity encounter, it's not so much that we bask in his or her glow, the way we might if our sibling won an award—it's more that we bask in the heat of a raging fire, gripped by a torrid fervor.

For some us, that feeling lingers our whole life. My grandfather used to talk about the time he met Albert Einstein at a party as if it were happening to him over and over again. Decades after the encounter he still felt an intimate connection to the great thinker because they had actually had a conversation, the way colleagues or friends might at a party, even if it was for only a few precious moments.

The Planned Celebrity Encounter

Of course the random encounter with a celebrity might be a bit too random for your liking. Never fear, celebrities (or their agents and publicists, at least) love nothing better than a line of adoring fans snaking out the door and around the block, waiting patiently for an autograph, a handshake, and a smile. To find out what drives fans to spend their whole day in line for a few precious moments with their favorite star, I went to the Virgin Megastore at New York's Union

Square, where scores of committed KISS fans had started lining up on the sidewalk early that morning. They were there for an appearance that evening by Peter Criss, founding member, drummer, and vocalist of the iconic rock group—you might know him best as "the Cat Man." He would be signing copies of his solo CD *One for All.*

Some fans had called in sick to be there; one was waiting in line for a solid day after clocking off his nightshift. Another guy, a forty-six-year-old schoolteacher, had come down from Toronto—about an eight-hour drive. He looked like a rank amateur compared to the twenty-seven-year-old who had trekked all the way from Melbourne, Australia—more than 10,000 miles—on a kind of KISS pilgrimage. For the last thirty-plus years and forty-five gold albums, the members of KISS have inspired the kind of fan devotion that many other bands can only dream about. Probably all those in the line agreed with Dave, who said: "KISS has been the soundtrack to my life."

Was the signing a way for these fans to feel closer to one of the founding members of KISS, to turn the illusion of intimacy into reality? A couple of the more hard-core fans—who each had KISS rooms at home, one displaying $45,000 worth of memorabilia, the other $100,000 worth—felt that if they had the chance to sit down with any of the members of KISS, they would definitely be friends. Others, though, didn't want to think of the members of the band that way. They looked a little horrified at the thought that they could be friends with the band members and said things like, "No! These guys are my *heroes.*"

But many felt a sense of brotherhood with the boys in the band. (Yeah, you guessed it, pretty much everyone in line was a guy. Oh, except for one little girl who came along with her father and was wearing a pastel pink T-shirt depicting each of the members of KISS in the guise of Hello Kitty . . . aww, cute!) Bob summed up the feeling of many of the fans when he said the members of KISS were "like brothers, because they have been there with me the whole time, through my life over the last thirty years."

Everyone was an avid watcher of *Gene Simmons Family Jewels*, a reality TV show that followed the life of the KISS guitarist and his family. What was interesting was that they watched every episode, even though they all agreed that it made Simmons look money hungry and just plain foolish. That didn't bother them at all. They said things like, "Oh, but that's just Gene for you," in a gentle tone, the way you might excuse an embarrassing but beloved relative who's just wrecked yet another public family outing.

Criss and Ace Frehley (the "Space Man") have both had well-documented battles with substance abuse, and yet many of the fans credited KISS with helping them fight their own demons and get through troubled periods of their lives. Dave said the reason for his devotion to the band was that "KISS has helped me through the hard times." Bob, now a successful sportswriter, said, "KISS has helped me get through some very bad personal troubles to now have a successful career, wife, and two children."

Mike, a fan since 1976, is covered in KISS tattoos. When asked how much of his time he spends on his devotion to the band, he immediately said, "One hundred percent of the day." He works as a delivery driver and plays KISS all day long in his truck, singing along; then he gets home and cranks up KISS on the stereo. Mike described following KISS as his "high."

I interviewed Peter Criss, a man renowned for keeping his life private. He told me he loves his fans and is glad that he can help them get through the tough times. His reponse to Mike? "Thank you for being a fan for so long; that's a safer high than drugs or alcohol."

Criss says that he maintains his privacy by not making many appearances or attending many public events. When he does meet fans, he tries to counteract whatever preconceptions they might have of him as a rock star by simply being himself, by "being real with them." He doesn't complain about the demands of fame but instead describes being on the receiving end of fans' attention as "wonderful, a dream come true, an overwhelming feeling."

When asked why so many complete strangers feel an intense closeness to him, he says, "I have a lot of fans who say they feel close to me because they can relate to me, or from my music I have helped them, so I feel it's from an emotional level. They feel close to me, and sometimes your feelings are not rational."

In fact, it seems that the old illusion of intimacy cuts both ways. Criss says, "Being a founding member of one of the most visually stimulating bands in rock and roll and having fans love you for so long, you can't help but feel intimacy with them, and I want to hold on to that for as long as I can.

"I will always feel KISS has the greatest fans in rock and roll."

And no doubt they would agree. Out there on the sidewalk at Union Square they caught up with friends they hadn't seen since the last KISS event, and they seemed genuinely at peace. One, trying to describe what it was like being among other fans, struggled to find the words, before it suddenly struck him: "You could actually say it is religious."

Why We Like to See Them Fall

So, we have an illusory intimacy with celebrities; we feel close and familiar with them. We get a thrill from seeing them or learning about even the most mundane aspects of their lives. We build them up, and we place them on a pedestal. Which all raises the question: Why do we love it so much when they topple off?

For ages you've kept track of a talented, gorgeous, rich young starlet who has three movies about to come out, a recording contract, and more houses than you have handbags. Then you see a story about her being totally trashed at a Hollywood hot spot, complete with a photo of her bleary-eyed self in the back of a limo. Maybe she was drunk, or maybe the paparazzi caught her midblink—you're not willing to condemn her yet. Then rumors about cocaine surface, along with whispers about a sex tape. When the starlet is arrested for DUI and goes to rehab for a month, you don't bother going to see her latest release at the cinema—you've decided you can wait until it's on cable. A couple of months later, when she drives the wrong way down the highway on a suspended license, you join the masses baying for her celebrity blood . . . well, calling for a prison term, at least.

When she drives the wrong way down the highway on a suspended license, you join the masses baying for her celebrity blood.

The weird thing is, you get as much—maybe even more—joy from reveling in the details of the starlet's demise as you did from watching her climb up the stairway to fame. The Germans have a term for this: *schadenfreude*—"pleasure taken from someone else's misfortune."

Schadenfreude is often directed to those in our *out-group*, because people tend to wish ill upon those who aren't like them. Human beings need to categorize things in order to make sense of the world. The minute we spot a new celebrity, we put them in a category, deciding if he or she should be in our in-group or our out-group. Is he or she attractive or unattractive to us? Does he or she share the same values as us, and behave the way we like people to behave? We compare the celebrity to our in-group and decide if he or she is like us or different from us (leaving aside a couple of obvious differences: his or her fame and wealth).

When a celebrity in our out-group fails in his or her career or is caught red-handed with six prostitutes and eleven ounces of cocaine, we take a small pleasure in that. Serves him or her right for not being more like us!

Envy can also be a strong motivator for schadenfreude, according to a recent study by Richard Smith published in the *Personality and Social Psychology Bulletin*. Not that we need a social psychologist to tell us this, as there are plenty of examples in everyday life. Let's say you work with an impossibly attractive woman who is continually being promoted, has a giant rock on her ring finger, is in the midst of planning a lavish wedding, and just won't shut up about how much her wonderful, rich, handsome fiancé treats her like a princess . . . and then he leaves her standing at the altar. You might not be proud of it, but for a split-second something inside you rejoices and does a little happy dance.

Now think about this in relation to celebrities. They parade by us with their entourage, with all of their bling, living a life of glitz and glamour. We are aware of all the expensive designer outfits they own, because we see them wearing them in magazines and on TV. The stars are so beautiful and iconic that they can make designers famous simply by wearing their clothes. They travel around the world on dream vacations and seem to spend every night in exclusive clubs and restaurants. It all looks so posh. We want that life, and we envy celebrities for having it. So when we find out that a celebrity has in fact *lost* it, the schadenfreude truly starts to flow.

In addition to being envious, I believe we find joy in stars' misfortunes because we resent the pressure to strive for a star-like lifestyle, which is unrealistic and unachievable for most. The idea that we should all aspire to wealth is deeply ingrained in our society. Most of us grew up hearing the message that we have to find a way to make a good living and that making money will somehow make us happy. The lesson is very general and unspecific; it's just, "Be rich." What does that mean? When we see all these images of the luxurious celebrity life, we say to ourselves, "Oh, *this* is what having money is all about." It helps us answer the question, "What am I supposed to be striving for?"

Media coverage of celebrities' glamorous, rich lives, along with celebrity advertising, put a lot of pressure on us to spend.

Media coverage of celebrities' glamorous, rich lives,

along with celebrity advertising, put a lot of pressure on us to spend. There are conflicting forces at work: We want to live like a celebrity, but we also resent our credit card bill each month. We blame the media, because celebrity and fashion magazines, TV shows, and increasingly even the news media are filled with tempting images of celebrity excess.

When a wealthy celebrity with a lifestyle we aspire to descends into substance abuse—or better yet, we hear he or she has filed for bankruptcy or been charged with tax evasion—we realize that he or she can't keep up with the celebrity lifestyle either. We are happy to see the celebrity fall, and we are relieved that fame and wealth aren't all they are cracked up to be. "If it ends in ruin and your business manager steals everything you have, then I don't want that life," we think to ourselves.

For the same reason, we love to see celebrity cellulite and stars without makeup. It makes them more real and takes the pressure off of us. Even though they have a personal trainer for each body part, a nutritionist for each meal, and a hair and makeup person at the ready, they can *still* look bad, so why on earth are we worrying?

David Levine, executive producer of CNN Headline News's *Showbiz Tonight*, sums it up: "People live the vicarious life through celebrities by following their stories. It's why [people] root for them when they're up." But when celebrities get too big, "people also get a cheap thrill because it makes them feel better there's somebody who's so rich and so powerful and so famous, like a Lindsay Lohan, and it happens to her too . . . she has the same addiction problems as we do." When stars fall, people can say, "See, I'm not so bad after all."

CHAPTER THREE

How Stars Are Created: The Machine

Above her, beneath her, and around her, the Machine hummed eternally; she did not notice the noise, for she had been born with it in her ears.

E. M. FORSTER, *THE MACHINE STOPS*

Try to picture a universe in which Demi Moore was Demetria Gene Guynes, algebra teacher. Or Johnny Depp, suburban bank manager. There's just something about stars that makes it seem as if they were born for fame, as if the high school yearbook picture of that 1980s perm existed for no other reason than to appear on an *E! True Hollywood Story*. Any day now, they'll find the gene for stardom, surely.

But scratch away at the glowing aura around celebrities and things begin to look a little less straightforward. A star isn't a star simply because of acting talent or good looks or an angelic singing voice. As fans, we may like to think that we're the ones who make celebrities; that *we* decide which actors, singers, or athletes to like. In fact there are other forces at work.

They call it the entertainment *industry* for a reason. Working behind the scenes is a whole team of people—movie-studio, record-company, and network executives; agents, managers, and promoters; marketers and advertising gurus; tabloid and magazine editors: the Machine. These are the people in the shadows, the ones who help decide who it is we will admire, who we will root for, and who we will pity. They are the ones who help decide who will become a celebrity.

Meet the Machine

The idea of puppet masters pulling the strings, of secret agencies at work in the wings, is not new. Just think of Yale University's Skull and Bones Society, which, since it was formed in the 1830s, has been said to have had a hand in selecting not only the university's student government but even state and federal governments. (George Bush and his son George W. are both known to have been members, as is John Kerry and a whole slew of high-profile lawmakers . . . I guess it's not *that* secret.)

The thought of mysterious agents controlling things in the background has long captured the imagination of writers, too. E. M. Forster's science fiction short story "The Machine Stops" imagines a world where everything is controlled by "the Machine," a force set in motion by man's own technology. When *Esquire* magazine did a cover story in 1992 about "the Machine," a Southern university secret society, the term entered everyday use. It became a way to describe all those people who devote their lives and careers to bringing one person to power or prominence. In the world of celebrity, it refers to the star makers—the handlers, agents, publicists, and everyone else who works hard in the background to make a celebrity a household name. No matter how talented he or she may be, no star can do it alone. Stars need the Machine to make it all happen.

The Actor's Agent

In the acting world, an all-important part of the Machine is the talent agent. This is the person whose job it is to spot the star-in-the-making amid the busloads of bright, shining young things arriving every day in Hollywood. Agents make the pivotal first connections with people who might one day help the wannabe star pay the rent: casting directors, producers, directors, and film and TV development folks. The agent gets his or her clients out to meetings with the people who matter and off to auditions for upcoming roles.

How do agents find work for their clients? Well, relationships for sure: Most deals in Hollywood are made because of personal introductions, or because a person, show, or movie is pitched through the agent's contacts. In addition, something the industry calls "breakdown" lands on agents' desks every day. This is a list of roles casting directors are holding auditions for. Mark Turner of the prestigious Abrams Artists Agency explains that the daily breakdowns "are mostly for films and acting roles for TV, with some commercials and some hosting thrown in." He says that while anyone can have access to breakdowns, "casting directors and producers tend to respond much better when a submission is made through an agent." So no matter what, for a prospective actor, getting on an agent's roster is important.

Robert Attermann is vice president of the Abrams Artists Agency and head of the theatrical department, which includes stage, television, and film. I asked him what the job of an agent is, and he told me, "Finding talent and getting them the right opportunities; also, negotiating deals and advising them why they should take project X over project Y, as well as choosing projects based on the people who are attached to them."

If anyone should know how to become famous it's Attermann, so I asked him how one goes about it (ya know, for your benefit, of course). He replied that it can actually be tricky when an actor on the agency's books shoots to fame and becomes a celebrity quickly. "Sometimes it just happens to them and we have to remind them to stay on the path and make the right choices," he said. That didn't really answer my question. I wanted to know, *How do I . . . I mean, does someone . . . become famous?* He said, "Everyone thinks they should be famous because they are watching the press of people like Paris Hilton and Lindsay Lohan, and they think it's cool. Shows like *Entourage* [which, by the way, he claims is quite a realistic depiction of the industry] and all of the reality shows send the message that anyone can be famous. They make it look like it's an easy thing to do." Sadly, he assures me, it isn't.

Agents are powerful, but even they have to acknowledge that there are some factors beyond the control of the Machine. Having talent, you'll be happy to hear, does have some bearing on an entertainer's chance for success. But some far more random factors can be just as important. According to Attermann, "The bottom line is certainly talent. The people who are talented will have longevity. That said, there are people out there who are incredibly talented but will never have the opportunity, unfortunately. Maybe they just don't have the look or are not at the right place at the right time. We have people who come in here and you would never guess they would ever go anywhere, then they book a TV series and it takes off from there and you couldn't have predicted it." I asked him how to get some of *that* kind of success. "Well," he said simply, "luck."

Attermann has seen firsthand that, talent aside, having someone who believes in you, plus luck, may be just what an actor needs in order to make it big versus fade away into oblivion: "Julia Roberts came in years ago and the commercial agent who met with her at the time said, 'Nah, she's too trailer park.' As a matter of fact, when we moved [offices] we were going through old rejection files and in there was Annette Benning, Robin Givens, Julia Roberts, and a couple of others."

The Music Biz

There are numerous cogs in the Machine if you want to become a musician—probably more than in any other area of the entertainment industry. They include the band's management, the music agent, the label, the tour manager, and the publicist, just to name a few. There is a lot of crossover among their roles, too, so there needs to be a delicate balance between each one.

New York–based music and entertainment publicist Jenn Nuccio explains, "The manager is responsible for making sure all the elements are together for their artist on a day-to-day basis. The agent, however, will have the role of booking an artist on a tour." It is incredibly important for an artist who is just starting out to have an agent, because "if it's an unknown band the agent will get them on a tour like, for example, Ozfest, or they may get them to open for an established band like Green Day." Another role the agent has is negotiating contracts on an artist's behalf, for instance for podcasts or TV endorsements deals.

Barbara Skydel, now of the legendary William Morris Agency, is probably one of the most prolific agents in the music industry. She and partner Frank Barcelona ran the influential agency Premier Talent, and together they discovered several now-huge acts and guided them through years of hard work to become the successful musicians they are today. On Skydel and Barcelona's résumé are, among others, U2, The Who, Tom Petty & The Heartbreakers, Journey, Roger Waters, The Pretenders, Bon Jovi, and Van Halen.

Skydel's talent is being able to hear something unique in an artist's sound that she knows will translate across cultures and generations. The perfect example is U2, whose global success has endured for almost three decades. "We signed them before the first record was out. We heard the music and said, 'This is fantastic.'. . . Sometimes you hear something and you just know."

> "We signed [U2] before the first record was out. . . . Sometimes you hear something and you just know."
>
> —BARBARA SKYDEL

Well who wouldn't know? Take one look into Bono's sultry blue eyes and how could you not hand him a contract, the keys to your summerhouse, and the rights to father your firstborn? This shows my post-MTV way of thinking and how shallow I am, because when Premier signed U2, it wasn't like that at all. "It was the music. We heard the music before we saw what they looked like. We didn't even know what they looked like."

This is one of the core differences between the music industry then and now, when looks are crucial to a musician's success. "The truth is, that all started with MTV—how you looked became important—but before MTV, artists were creating something that a lot of those MTV acts couldn't duplicate on stage." Growing up as I have in a pop-culture, celebrity-driven, looks-oriented world, I cannot imagine the freedom that musicians must have felt when it didn't matter what they looked like. Skydel tells me, "The first time I saw the Jefferson Airplane, they didn't even face the audience! They played with their backs to the crowd, they were dressed in the clothes that they woke up in that morning, and it didn't matter what people looked like. You didn't have to have your teeth fixed, your hair colored, or whatever you do now. The only thing that mattered was your songwriting ability and your performing ability. When MTV came in, it really changed all that."

I commented to Barbara Skydel that I think something else has changed in the music industry, too: It seems easier to become a star, thanks to *American Idol*. She tried to disavow me of my bias: "*American Idol* is just a quicker way to get there, but if a person's got the goods it depends on their own limitations, how far they can go with it, what is the marketplace, and who's behind them." And if they don't have real talent and are instead created by the *AI* machine, with nothing substantial to back it up, they "might not have a long shelf life."

Constantine Maroulis, who as an *American Idol* finalist in 2005 has an insider's viewpoint, agrees with Skydel. As he sees it, the major benefit to a singer's career from appearing on *Idol* is that a record label might look at a contestant and think, "Maybe they didn't win, but they've been on TV and millions of people do like them and have been voting for them . . . and wow, it's a great training program. They are a better performer, they're seasoned already—what most people go through in thirty years they've gone through in thirty days."

But future success depends on putting in the effort. "I grew up in the theater," says Maroulis, "so I understand the progression and the hard work involved and am not afraid to do what it takes to work my way up, like from ensemble to leading role when you are a Broadway guy. . . . It's a blue collar mentality. It's about the job and not the bull. Millions of actors are not working, and there are plenty of singers who have no record deals."

"If you start out wanting to be a celebrity, you're in big trouble."

—BARBARA SKYDEL

So I asked Skydel to explain how one becomes a celebrity in the music industry. (Not that I have *any* talent, but just in case one day singing off key and being tone deaf is in.) She explained, "If you start out wanting to be a celebrity, you're in big trouble." This is advice that young artists need to heed, given that every music insider I speak with says that on a regular basis they have potential clients walk in stating that they "want to be famous" and that's about it.

According to Skydel, "To start out, you have to have a passion for what you are doing, and the passion is in the art. It's in songwriting and performing. This industry is *hard* work." She offers words of caution to those whose sole goal is to become a big star: "For those who make it, celebrity is an outgrowth of what happens to them, and many artists don't look for celebrity. They don't look to be chased by paparazzi, and they don't look to never have a personal life. Instead, they have a life of art, and to some the unfortunate part of it is the celebrity part, where they no longer have a private existence out of the public eye."

Darryll Brooks, a promoter and artist manager, has been a big part of the Machine since the early 1970s, managing the careers and promoting the live shows of acts such as Prince, Stevie Wonder, Earth Wind and Fire, Ray Parker, Parliament-Funkadelic, Run-DMC, Salt-N-Pepa, Kid 'n Play, and Mya. Brooks goes on his gut instinct when he meets a potential artist, and, as with a love connection, relies on chemistry. "I look for artists I'm compatible with. I've had record labels like Interscope and Sony send me people that they were interested in, but if the chemistry isn't there, it's not going to work." Like Attermann, he recognizes the role that finding the right backer at the right time plays in the making of a star. "Jimmy Iovine [who formed Interscope Records, famous for launching Tupac, No Doubt, Nine Inch Nails, and later Death Row Records] had a tape laying around that Dr Dre picked up, and it happened to be Eminem. Dre is one of those amazing producers who can hear something and it grabs them in a certain way." But, says Brooks, a star's fortunate break can just as easily come to nothing. "It can turn over like the seasons. A guy at a label really believes in an artist, but then he gets fired and the new people aren't interested."

Brooks makes a clear distinction between talented musicians whose careers have longevity and those who are solely celebrities. He says there is a science to building character and integrity in the music industry: "That's why you have artists who are still around after all these years; their connection grows as the audience does." Prince, who has been a highly respected and popular performer for thirty years, is a great example, according to Brooks. "He writes music, sings well, and tells a story that brings you into the character." Celebrity is another beast, Brooks believes, and has nothing to do with real talent and staying power as an artist. In his many years in the industry, he has seen the rise and fall of many "stars" who really weren't the talent behind their hits but simply what he calls "puppets."

> "Most of these performers who can't perform are just puppets of producers and computers. Record labels keep manufacturing them because it's a business."
>
> —DARRYLL BROOKS

"We glamorize celebrity more than any other entity," says Brooks. "Most of these performers who can't perform are just puppets of producers and computers. Record labels keep manufacturing them because it's a business. They need to keep making them up. Which one is the shiniest? And then it becomes like going down to a used car lot: 'Paint it red, send it out, we need three more red ones.'"

Sometimes a genuine star, a supernova, breaks through all the noise with something to say or a fresh sound, which then becomes the "it" thing.

On seeing this star's success, the Machine tries to manufacture more of the same. As Brooks says, "When something works, like the Supremes for example, all the record companies mimic the formula. 'Its time for an all-female group,' and they keep doing it until that one falls off the vine. Then it's like, here we go again."

The Publicity Machine

Another vital cog in the Machine is the media—magazines, tabloids, radio, TV, and the galaxy of Web sites and blogs devoted to celebrities. Actor, author, and musician Stephen Collins notes, "The whole present-day celebrity culture barely existed when I was starting out in the early 1970s. Keep in mind that there was no *People* magazine, no *Us*, no E!, no *ET*, no *Insider*, no cable TV, and most people were embarrassed to be caught looking at the *National Enquirer*, even in the supermarket."

Attermann adds, "There are so many more channels now and so many more places where people can become famous. The amount of channels we have has more than doubled. It used to be just ABC, NBC, and CBS; now there are so many channels—UPN, the CW, Lifetime, TNT, FX, Showtime, HBO [to name a few]—and there is some great programming on all of those channels." And some not so great—but regardless, while TV channels proliferate, the celebrity-gossip magazines, TV shows, and Web sites proliferate, too.

This profusion of media outlets means not only more television, film, and YouTube roles for those who want to become stars, it also means more opportunities for us to get our daily gossip jones. And the celebrity-gossip media is a star factory. How do you know that someone is a celebrity, that this is a person you should pay attention to? You know because you see his or her image splashed on every celebrity-gossip magazine while you're standing in line at the supermarket, or you regularly catch sight of them posing on the red carpet or on *Extra* or the *Insider.* Media attention is like oxygen to stars' careers.

While sometimes it may seem that stars spend their days trying to escape the paparazzi, they know that they *need* the media—to sell their image or their latest movie, TV show, album, perfume, clothing line, and so on. This is where the publicist steps in, to help the star navigate his or her way through the sometimes vicious world of the media. Much the way agents provide actors with connections to producers, directors, and studios, publicists provide connections with the right magazine and newspaper editors and radio and TV producers. They know how to sell the star's story and put the star in the best light. They know how to court controversy, capture headlines, and run damage control.

Publicist Susan Blond, a protégé of Andy Warhol and a giant in the music industry, has represented some of the biggest celebrities. You'll want names, I'm guessing. Okay, but you might want to put on some hefty shoes, because I'm about to drop a lot of them. Susan has helped package, polish, and promote the public image of everyone from Janet and Michael Jackson, Britney Spears, the Osbournes, Usher, LL Cool J, Snoop Dogg, P. Diddy, and Nelly to the Clash, Duran Duran, and David Bowie; she has worked with Prince, and she's worked with Star Jones (during her hardest times, I may add).

I asked her how she takes an unknown talent and turns him or her into a household name. "Get them that first buzz, the first column. . . . You are working with a career, and you want them to be happy with the choices you've made. It can go from a little line in a paper where you're just the expert, to a big feature in *Vanity Fair,* to cover stories or a TV show."

The best example of Blond building the profile of a star is the young Michael Jackson, with whom she worked early on in his solo career. "I worked with Michael Jackson for about thirteen years and then again in 2001 for the thirtieth anniversary [of his first single as a solo act]." She understands the power that the publicist wields: "If people are very, very talented and are very interesting, and they're entertainers, we can get them their dreams."

But even Michael Jackson had to struggle through it for a while; it was not until his fifth solo album, *Off the Wall*, that anyone really knew who he was. Even though *Off the Wall* sold seven million copies in the United States, Susan still had to persuade *Rolling Stone* to put Michael on the cover. "Getting him on that cover was very tough, because people from *Rolling Stone* would sit with me, the editors, who said, 'It's not our audience,' and it wasn't until you could convince them, 'Yes, this is your audience now, and this is bigger than whoever you think your audience is. The world wants to hear about Michael Jackson.'"

Sometimes clients know what they want, and they can dictate to their publicists what to do. Janet Jackson was one such client. "When I met with Janet, she'd say, 'I just wanna be in the columns," . . . and she wanted sixty things in those columns. She just wanted to keep hot, and that's what she wanted—to just keep that name on 'Page Six.'" ('Page Six' is the quintessential gossip column in the *New York Post.* It is said to be where the celebrities and Hollywood insiders have always turned for the best gossip. Technically, it has been on page ten or even page twelve for the past five years, yet it is still referred to as 'Page Six.' If your name appears there, you are *somebody.*)

Think Like a Star

One of the Machine's tried-and-true techniques is to have a would-be celebrity simply adopt the mantle of a star. Behave like a star, think like a star, and create an atmosphere of glamour and importance around you, and you just might convince enough people you *are* a star.

> "They hired kids to create a hysteria and appear to be fans running after them, to bring out the look of folks running after the star."
>
> —DARRYLL BROOKS

This tool has been used to great effect in the music industry. Brooks says that early in his career "the Jacksons were doing a pictorial for *Ebony* magazine, and they hired kids to create a hysteria and appear to be fans running after them, to bring out the look of folks running after the star. Readers didn't know it was staged." Music insiders also hired fake fans to rush the stage as they were arriving at concerts. "It was to hype the image," Brooks says.

Actor Stephen Collins has been a celebrity and a fly on the wall for many major events in entertainment. He believes there is an element of choice in becoming a high-profile celebrity who is hounded by paparazzi and obsessive fans. In his view being a successful entertainer doesn't necessarily mean you *have* to become the kind of celebrity we see plastered all over the tabloids on a daily basis. "I've known and worked with countless huge stars and found that they can pretty much all be divided into two groups: those who—at least subconsciously—desperately need the ego gratification that comes from being noticed wherever they go, and those who get over themselves and move quietly through the world attracting little attention. It's a conscious decision that one has to make."

Collins, who worked with Jessica Biel for nearly ten years on his show *7th Heaven*, goes on to recall: "I worked with Robert Redford when he was pretty much at the height of his fame. He just walked down Fifth Avenue in New York, and there's something about him that says, 'Yeah, it's me. No big deal. You don't have to make a fuss.' No bodyguards, no entourage. And people left him alone. I've known others, who shall remain nameless, who just seemed to invite people to notice them and make a fuss. I mean, if you walk around the streets of Manhattan with a phalanx of bodyguards, as I once saw a big star do—six bodyguards surrounding him—people wonder who the hell it is and *need* to know, to see more, to get closer."

Platinum-selling singer-songwriter Edwin McCain has garnered the attention of millions with his top-ten smash "I'll Be" and the Diane Warren–penned top-forty hit "I Could Not Ask for More." His songs get a lot of wedding play and radio airtime and are perennial favorites of *American Idol* contestants year after year. He believes that when it comes to fame and celebrity, there are two ways to go about achieving it: "Work the media and develop this notion of fame and act famous so in turn [you] become famous, or like Ani DiFranco, where you say, 'Fame and celebrity are not real,' so you reject it, and in that rejection you become famous to those who agree with your point of view and become more and more popular among the proletariat of folks who agree with you and your artistic endeavor. The crowd seems to swell when that happens."

McCain tells a great story about David Bowie, when he was just starting to be recognized. "When Bowie and his manager came to New York, they were riding around in a limo wearing furs, staying at the Waldorf, creating the image that he was a star, even though they were flat broke. It was a 'fake-it-till-you-make-it' mentality, and then the perception becomes the reality. All you need to do is project what you want to be true, and sometimes it does—and sometimes it doesn't, which is why fame can only carry you so far, and then the music has to be good. Your music has to speak for itself; celebrity is fleeting, music is lasting."

> "Your music has to speak for itself; celebrity is fleeting, music is lasting."
>
> —EDWIN MCCAIN

In McCain's case, the Machine did not start working until he made a name for himself on his own. "I was turned down nine billion times and kept on pounding away until someone said 'Yes.' I played show after show after show; I was not to be denied."

Once he achieved fame, he experienced what he calls "the curse of the famous." He says this means that deep down you don't believe the compliments and adulation that other people give you. "You feel it's both untrue and unreal, and think, 'I don't deserve to be here,'" he says. McCain has now matured into a musician as opposed to a celebrity, but he does admit that at first he did buy in to the whole fame thing. He had several humbling moments that snapped him back to reality. "I remember when my song was number five on the charts, the Atlantic [Records] representative and a major radio programmer took me to Sky Bar—at the time it was *the* place to go in LA. We go up to the big bouncer guy at the velvet rope to get into the club and the rep says, 'Do you know who this is?' and he said, 'I know who he is; he's not on the list.'"

Become a "Brand"

Übermanager Benny Medina, one of the most famous star makers of the past decade—and the real-life inspiration for *The Fresh Prince of Bel-Air,* which he coproduced—knows that the secret to creating an intergalactic level of stardom is branding. Here's how you know when an entertainer is in the good hands of Medina: He or she is more than just a "singer" or an "actor"; he or she is a franchise, a brand. Medina is credited with "creating" Jennifer Lopez, Will Smith, Brandy, Tyra Banks, and others.

He made Jennifer Lopez more than just a dancer—he made her a singer whose albums have sold millions; an actress (despite what you may think of her acting ability, she's been in more films than you have); a television producer (of the reality show *Dance Life*); an entrepreneur with her own clothing line, perfume, and restaurant; and the spokesperson for everyone from L'Oreal to Louis Vuitton. In 1999 I was at a party Medina was throwing for Lopez's debut album *On the 6* (a reference to the 6 train she used to take up to the Bronx when she really was "Jenny from the block"). It was at a small club in downtown New York City . . . but before I continue, I should probably tell you I was not one of the distinguished guests but was there because my mother had organized the event and I was her assistant for the night. Everyone who was anyone in the radio and music industry was there for this listening party, the aim of which was to encourage stations to add her single "If You Had My Love" to their playlists. It was a magical night, and when the guest of honor arrived in her tight salmon-pink leather skirt and beautiful shimmery sequined top and flipped her hair in my face, I didn't care. Instead I was in awe of Medina and the folks he had assembled for this musical coming-out party. To see the Machine operating in all its glory—turning a then moderately successful actress and dancer into an all-round superstar—was really something.

Publicist Susan Blond tells me that Russell Simmons was really the first entertainment entrepreneur to grasp the opportunity to create a multifaceted brand. "When we represented Russell, he already had the *Def Comedy Jam* [an HBO series showcasing the work of African-American comics], he had the beginnings of Phat Farm clothing, he had a movie company, and he managed to *be* the record company [Def Jam]. He was one of the first, and now everyone does it." Simmons sold Phat Farm in 2004 for a reported $140 million. He has added everything from "author" (of a self-help book, in 2007) and financier (he has a line of Baby Phat credit cards) to the Simmons brand.

Simmons may have been the first to realize that the artist can be more than just a musician, but he wasn't the first to connect music with an existing brand in order to generate publicity, brand loyalty, and—let's face it—capital. According to Brooks, that honor may go to Run-DMC. In 1986, way before Simmons's Phat Farm and associated branding, Brooks was helping to make Run-DMC's song "My Adidas" (the hip-hop trio were big fans of the sports shoes) much more than a music track. "Russell is a very unique commodity because he paid attention to more than just one thing," says Brooks, "but we did a promotion in Baltimore during the *Raising Hell* tour with Run-DMC called 'Show Your Adidas,' and this was the beginning of what branding was all about. The kids all came wearing Adidas, took them off, and raised them in the air. It was incredible and it blew everybody away."

This may have been the first time a brand and a group shared synchronicity, and it paid off for everyone. "Adidas gave the group money and a necklace with a speaker to wear around their necks. It's clear that when you represent a certain demographic, those companies want to pay attention." Adidas continues to benefit from the association, still using the brand's connection to Run-DMC in its marketing campaigns.

Since then, everyone has cashed in; it's a trend that has kept on keeping on. According to Brooks, "Everyone who came through Def Jam came from that same camp." He cites rapper Jay-Z, who in 1995 cofounded the fashion label *Rocawear*, which has annual retail sales over $700 million; and Beanie Sigel, a hip-hop artist who epitomizes the celebrity-as-brand concept by having a fashion label, State Property Wear (a subsidiary of Rocawear), named after his group, State Property. Rappers from other labels also know how to brand themselves on a scale never seen before. Sean "Diddy" Combs's clothing line, Sean John, captures an estimated $400 million of the $42 billion we spend to look good each year.

We are more apt to buy into the brand if we like the celebrity. As Blond says, "Celebrities become everything to people." As a case in point she uses her client Napoleon Perdis, whose cosmetics line is featured at Target and was chosen as the official makeup sponsor of the Fifty-ninth Primetime Emmy Awards in 2007. "You don't buy anything until your favorite star wears it. . . . If you want the girl down the street to buy it, it helps that Charlize Theron wears [Napoleon's] makeup."

Celebrities license their name, market themselves the same way a company would sell a widget, and keep their image front and center. Blond has even begun to see the branding trend in her youngest clients. "When I meet with thirteen-year-olds now they all want to be 'brands,'" she says.

When I asked Maroulis if he has any advice for young people who want to become stars, branding is definitely on the top of his list. "Even with the record companies, it's not about selling just a record," he says. "It's about merchandise, ringtones, etc.—they supplement lack of record sales with other things. The music industry is not what it used to be. Look at Justin Timberlake. He has his clothing line and restaurants."

This trend toward the entertainer becoming the multitasking entrepreneur may explain why we use the word *celebrity* so often now. It is a catchall term that can describe so many levels and types of stardom. Take the Olsen twins, for example—Mary-Kate and Ashley. They rose to fame as child actors in the TV show *Full House* and have gone on to star in movies, but would you call them simply actors? Not really, because they are so much more. Take a quick look at their Web site (www.mary-kateandashley.com) and you'll find that tween fans can purchase a mind-boggling array of merchandise from the Olsen twin empire: jackets, tops, pants, underwear, shoes, sunglasses, iPod cases, lip gloss, fragrance, the twins' DVDs and books, handbags, floor rugs, and more. In fact the Web site covers just about every conceivable aspect of a girl's life: personal advice, beauty tips, horoscopes, and the skinny on what clothes she should be wearing this season, movies she should be watching this month, and songs she should be listening to this week. She can even go deep with "Today's Thought" from the twins. (Okay, maybe not *that* deep if "Give yourself a spring manicure. Paint your nails a cool new color!" is anything to go by. But you get the idea.) *Mogul* might be a more appropriate term for the Olsens, but somehow that just doesn't do the trick, either. *Celebrity* seems to fit just right.

But while Mary-Kate and Ashley have worked hard for years to establish acting careers and are clearly astute businesswomen, the term *celebrity* has also become synonymous with people who are famous yet have no distinguishable talent whatsoever, people who are famous for simply being famous. Does being in the tabloids make you a celebrity? Does scandal? Does being called a "celebrity" sometimes mean little more than "You're in the public eye, but we can't categorize you, so we'll lump you into that grab bag called 'celebrity'"?

Pop culture expert Jarett Weiselman breaks it all down: "The term *celebrity* has become so all encompassing; everybody—from a D-list reality star to Jessica Simpson, who has so much going on [the clothing line, the acting, the singing, the hair extensions she licenses, etc.]— falls under the same umbrella term of *celebrity*. The term has become so watered down that there is no distinction between the A-list star and the D-list nobody, which is why *celebutant* became a new term [which combines the words *celebrity* and *debutante* and describes people such as the Hiltons and distinguishes them from those such as the Olsens]. This understanding of the word *celebrity* also explains why so many people feel they can become celebrities. One could apply the term to someone doing even the minimal amount of work." Just so long as they do it in the public eye.

Oprah can no longer be classified a "talk show host," as she runs not only her own TV show but also a production company, magazine, and philanthropic school for girls in South Africa. She's a celebrity. But so are the latest reality-show participants who share little in common with Oprah but the skill of multitasking. Since their show finished, they might have spun a career out of going to nightclub openings or commentating on other reality shows. They might not get the same amount of respect and admiration as Oprah, but for a time at least, they may get the same amount of column inches in the paper and the same attention from TV and radio stations. It's no wonder that for a growing number of people, celebrity looks like an easy thing to achieve and something that they, too, deserve.

Part Two

The Impact the Cult of Celebrity Has on Our Lives

CHAPTER FOUR

Fourteen Minutes and Counting

If you come to fame not understanding who you are, it will define who you are.

OPRAH WINFREY

When I was four years old, I made a very important career decision: I was going to be a ballerina. I was not like the other kids in my class, who were choosing between fairy princess and unicorn. I was in tap, jazz dance, and ballet class with my friend Debbie, and we were going to the top.

By the time I reached the ripe old age of six, I had abandoned my dreams of the American Ballet Theater for the simple farm life of horse doctor. (Which was odd since I lived in a city where the nearest horse farm was well over 250 miles away.) Then at ten I declared I would someday coach the Pittsburgh Steelers. Chuck Noll had to retire sometime. I may have been a girl, but I was also the son my mother never had. I was a total jock, and while I thought it might be a problem getting into the locker room as a woman and all, it was a barrier I was willing to break. I never considered that football coaches were indeed ex-football players. And that's the key to achieving your dreams: knowing what it takes to actually do whatever it is you want to do. My dream of "football coach" was dashed when I learned that I would need to play for the NFL, or at least be a star college football player. Not so realistic at 5 feet, 2 inches and 105 pounds . . . oh yeah, and a girl.

My friend Debbie thought she would easily make the jump from ballerina to astronaut. Too bad she didn't stick with it, because that dream wasn't so far-fetched. It would have required going to graduate school to get her doctorate in aeronautics, accompanied by years of piloting or military experience. Then she could apply to NASA's space program and maybe one day become an astronaut. Had she followed that trajectory, she might have been on her way into space.

It isn't like that in the entertainment industry. There is no such clear linear path to success. You can't do A, B, and C and then end up at job D. Interview fifty celebrities and they will give you fifty different stories as to how they got where they are. And for each one who makes it to the height of stardom, there are thousands who fall away, giving up their dream after years of spending all their hard-earned cash on singing or acting coaches, schlepping to auditions, recording demo tapes, and meeting endless rejection. Let's face it: The vast majority of people who seek fame and fortune are about as likely to ever deliver an Oscar or Grammy acceptance speech as I am to deliver the halftime motivational speech in the Steelers' locker room.

So why is it that greater numbers of young people than ever before believe that they can—and should—be famous? Why has "celebrity" become a career goal, and why are so many young people (even those with meager talents) willing to give themselves to the pursuit of stardom?

The Emerging Adults

In May 2000, Jeffrey Jensen Arnett, Ph.D., published an article in a journal called *American Psychologist,* the psychology equivalent of *Playboy* in that when it arrives we can't wait to open it up because we know something juicy will be inside; it is psychology porn (that we read for the articles, of course). In it he described a new generation of kids in their late teens through twenties, the eighteen to thirty set, which he called the "emerging adults." He became a rock star in the world of psychology for coining a term, spawning new research, and identifying something important happening in our culture.

Over the past thirty years, the concept of adulthood has changed. The transition from adolescence to adulthood has become prolonged, and young people are moving back home after college and marrying later in life. Increasing numbers are choosing careers such as movie actress or pop star. Many are extending their education rather than entering the workforce—or rejecting formal schooling and going for singing or acting lessons instead. Amoung other career ambitions, many emerging adults want to be famous.

Entitled to Fame

If you are skeptical about that statement, consider the research of psychologist Jean Twenge. In her fourteen-year study, 16,475 college students nationwide completed a questionnaire designed to assess where they ranked in the personality trait of narcissism. This is one of the few personality traits that psychologists judge to be largely negative, as it features self-focused behavior, arrogance, a sense of entitlement, and a lack of empathy and concern for others. Twenge and her colleagues found that two-thirds of the students rated above average in narcissism. As you can imagine, Twenge made headlines with these findings. They signaled that there had been an enormous shift in the personalities of an entire generation, often referred to as Gen Y. "College students think they're *so* special," one headline read. "Big Babies: Think the Boomers are self-absorbed? Wait until you meet their kids," read another.

Twenge also found that the emerging adults' higher rating in narcissism was linked to an increased desire to be famous. In her book *Generation Me: Why Today's Young Americans Are More Confident, Assertive, Entitled—and More Miserable than Ever Before*, she says, "Many kids today grow up thinking that they will eventually be movie stars, sports figures, or at least rich . . . a lot of young people also assume that success will come quickly."

An alarming number of kids believe they will "likely be famous at whatever career they choose."

In my own research for my master's thesis, I found that an alarming number of kids believe they will "likely be famous at whatever career they choose." And most of the research done today finds that more than half of the emerging adult population feels that way.

This may explain why so many emerging adults are choosing to delay the responsibilities of work and family until later on. Decades ago many people in that age group might have been setting up their own homes and families, but studies show that now most eighteen- to twenty-five-years-olds do not yet consider themselves to be adults. And if you don't yet consider yourself an adult, you can do things like audition for *American Idol* over and over or take acting classes in the middle of the day.

"You feel entitled to get the best in life: the best clothes, the best house, the best car. You're special; you deserve special things."

—JEAN TWENGE

One mother I interviewed for this book told me about a friend's daughter who did just that—auditioned for *American Idol.* I asked how far the girl got, to which she replied, "She made it to Hollywood. Simon really liked her, but then she was cut." And then she added, "She still thinks she's going to be a star."

"Oh," I said, "is she taking singing lessons or going on auditions? Did she sign with a label, that sort of thing?"

"No. So far she is still waiting to be discovered. She doesn't want to work, it's not the life she's accustomed to, so she's living at home and hoping that someone will find her. It's been four years so far."

This girl is not alone. There are kids in their teens and early twenties who feel they deserve to be "found" and that they don't need to do anything to make it happen. And why not live that way? Their parents aren't kicking them out anytime soon. Over the past thirty years there has been a steadily increasing trend for people in the eighteen to thirty age group to live with their parents. The most recent research shows that over eighteen million emerging adults—or 40 percent of single people in that age range—have moved back home. Higher housing costs and lower wages for entry-level jobs have contributed to this trend, but several experts cite something else. For example, Twenge, whose latest book is *The Narcissism Epidemic,* argues that it is because emerging adults will not settle for second best. She writes: "You feel entitled to get the best in life: the best clothes, the best house, the best car. You're special; you deserve special things."

On my radio show one night a twenty-five-year-old caller agreed. He said, "Why should I have a not-so-nice car and a crummy apartment, when I can live in my parents' beautiful house with good food and clean towels? It wouldn't be as nice if I lived on my own. Why should I spend my hard-earned money on bills and rent when I can just move home?"

Stars Don't Have to Grow Up

In two studies, one conducted by Jeffrey Arnett and another by researcher Frederick Lopez, people age eighteen to twenty-five were asked to define what it means to be an adult. For example, is it financial freedom from parents, or being married and running a household? Is it chronological age? Does it mean you have to stop partying?

The researchers found that for people in that age group, adulthood is mostly about being in control of one's emotions, dealing with critical life events, and making mature career decisions—all milestones that typically take place somewhere near the age

Ban freeloading. If you have a child over eighteen still living at home who is waiting to be discovered by a talent scout—and his or her technique basically involves watching a lot of TV, talking on the cell phone, and doing two shifts a week at the local video store—it's time to make that child take some responsibility. All kids need to learn life skills and to learn to be independent, as they will eventually have to move out on their own. You are not doing them any favors by coddling them if deep down you don't believe there is a future star sitting on your couch playing X-Box.

Many stars cite their parents as being their greatest mentors and supporters in the early part of their career, and they say it was their parents' faith and sacrifices that assured their success. But these are celebrities such as Tyra Banks, Katherine Heigl, Beyoncé Knowles, Charlize Theron—people who worked incredibly hard, but who also had natural ability that was undeniable right from the start. It's more than fine to be there to support your child's attempt to make it in the entertainment industry—so long as he or she is doing his or her share of the heavy lifting.

of thirty. Calling this population "young adult" is wrong, they argued, since they do not yet consider themselves adults—that's why the term "emerging adult" is more appropriate.

The reality is that people in this age group have yet to contend with the results of their own decision making, nor have they reaped the benefits of their choices. Viewed from this perspective, the fact that some people in the eighteen to thirty age group think it's okay to wait to be "found" and turned into a star makes sense: They haven't yet had to pay the rent or a mortgage, squirrel away retirement savings, or put their own kids through college.

To these not-yet-ready-to-be-adults, the world of fame must seem especially appealing, given that immaturity in stars is not just forgiven but almost celebrated. Case in point: the celebrity tantrum. Many celebrity icons, regardless of their chronological age, are renowned for appearing incredibly immature and throwing temper tantrums whenever they don't get their way. There is Burt Reynolds's slap heard round the world at the premiere of the remake of *The Longest Yard* (Reynolds is said to have slapped a reporter in the face for not having seen the original version, which starred . . . Burt Reynolds); Kanye West's childish rant at the MTV Video Music Awards in 2007 (he was angry for not receiving any awards or being asked to be the opening act for the show); and countless incidents of stars lashing out at paparazzi (of which a nationwide favorite must be the sight of a bald-headed Britney bashing a car with an umbrella).

Everyone will cater to your every need, just as a mother would for her toddler. It's one of the draws of celebrity.

Then there are the temper tantrums that happen behind the scenes. When Sean Combs was Puff Daddy—or maybe he was

"Puffy," I can't keep up—he called his publicist, Susan Blond, before New York's Fashion Week to request a seat at the Versace show. "He said if we didn't get him in, we would be fired," says Blond. "We called, but it was the middle of this East Coast–West Coast rap war when everyone was being shot." The organizers didn't want any trouble and had decided that the only fair thing to do was to avoid inviting rappers from either the East Coast or the West Coast camps, "so they didn't want him, and we were fired the next day." Despite the fact that this was a good publicist who worked hard, she was let go in the blink of an eye. This sort of immature behavior is indicative of what celebrity is all about: You get to be a big baby whenever you want to because everyone will cater to your every need, just as a mother would for her toddler. It's one of the draws of celebrity.

The emerging adults see celebrities their age, and older, living in a kind of suspended adolescence, not having to deal with all the boring stuff in life—getting up at the same time every day when the alarm goes off, commuting down a congested highway, remembering to pay the cell phone bill. Instead, they see images of celebrities studded with jewels at red-carpet events, hanging out at clubs midweek, and playing with their toys (luxury cars, pedigree lapdogs, class A drugs, etc.) in the schoolyard (LA, New York).

How appealing it all must look to emerging adults. Never mind what they don't see: That for most stars it took a lot of effort to get where they are, and their lives are plagued by neuroses. ("Where is the next acting job coming from?" "Do my fans still love me?" "Why isn't my single selling?" "Am I starting to look old?" "Is my manager trying to rip me off?") They don't see the hard work that goes into making movies or albums or what it takes to write a hit song. They don't know what it's like to get rejected time after time at casting calls or be a nobody touring the country 300 nights a year until a label finally signs you.

Shows such as *American Idol* can appear to bless young performers with sudden fame. But what viewers don't see is the years of hard work that went into their "overnight" success. Take 2005 finalist Constantine Maroulis. Before *Idol*, he earned a degree at the prestigious Boston Conservatory and then, he says, "I went back to New York, where I am from, and was lucky enough to land a role in the touring company of [the musical] *Rent*. So I went out on the road with *Rent*, playing the lead role. At the time I also had a band and I was just hustling, like you do."

Maroulis was working so hard out on the road that while he knew of *American Idol*, he hadn't actually seen the show. It was a former girlfriend who encouraged him to audition. He approached that audition not as if it would be his ticket to instant stardom, but the way he did any other gig a working performer might try out for. "I approached it like it was every other audition," he says.

Viewers don't see how the stars have struggled. Instead they see the glamorous end result—and they want *that*. The illusion is that celebrity is an easy, luxurious life where you feel special all the time—and that is just the kind of thing that many emerging adults have grown up believing they need and deserve.

An Army of Me

The emerging adults' need for fame has been encouraged by their parents, who tell them how talented they are, whether they have any real talent or not. Twenge found that the increased level of narcissism in college students is due to parents raising their kids to be "special" and telling them that they can be whatever they want to be—without emphasizing the necessary

Get strategic. To you emerging adults out there who have decided that, yes, a career as a performer and celebrity is what you really want: It's time to get strategic. Are there any classes you can take to help you on the way? How are your networking skills? How many hours a day can you devote to practicing your craft? If you need some money to follow your dream, what skills do you have—or can you develop—to get a job? Have you got any contacts you can call to help you break into the industry?

It's also time to be specific about your goals. "I want to be famous" is not enough to make a true vocation. Celebrity might look like one big endless party, but a long-term career in the entertainment industry is hard work, and you need to be sustained by something deeper, such as a love of the craft of performing.

hard work and talent. The motive of these parents isn't a bad one: Their aim is to raise their children's self-esteem. But, as Twenge notes, they are going about it the wrong way and are creating self-esteem based on a "shaky foundation." The emerging adults are an entire generation who won awards for just showing up, because everyone is equal; they were given little incentive to be smarter or, heaven forbid, make mistakes and learn coping skills. This is the same generation whose educators did away with gifted programs because they were unfair to average kids.

When I was just starting out, there was a girl in my circle who so desperately wanted to be a singer—no, a pop star. She worked some of the crummiest jobs at the worst of hours to support her "craft," as she always referred to it. She spent every cent she had on vocal coaches, headshots, cute pop-star outfits, and plastic surgery. When she finally got enough money together to produce her own CD, she held a party at her parents' place (where she was living at age twenty-five) to showcase her unique talent. She invited everyone she knew, and she asked along a local newspaper music reviewer to document this momentous occasion. We all turned out for her musical debut to the world—after all, wouldn't you have wanted to be there when Christina Aguilera sang her first note?

She got up on a makeshift stage in her backyard and made a speech thanking us for coming and her parents for their support and promising that she wouldn't forget us when she was famous. Everybody was shaking with anticipation, the CD began, and you could hear by the first note that it was horrible—no, *excruciating*. I would have preferred forty minutes of the emergency broadcast signal tone. I looked over at her parents and they were just overjoyed and beaming—I think I even saw a couple of tears—as though their little girl deserved to make it big and here she was finally achieving that goal. Later I overheard her mother talking to the reporter: "Isn't she incredible? Like Mariah Carey [more like Drew Carey]. My baby has perfect pitch!"

My young friend—who, needless to say, has not made it big—was an early example of those children who feel entitled to fame and special treatment because their parents conditioned them that way. She—like the emerging adult population today—would have benefited from parents who were a little more, um, realistic.

But instead of realism and guidance, what many of the current generation of emerging adults get from their parents is an echoing of their own immaturity.

In his best seller, *Balsamic Dreams: A Short but Self-Important History of the Baby Boomer Generation,* Joe Queenan sardonically describes his thought process when he has a cancer scare (which luckily turns out to be just that, a scare). His reaction to what he fears is his imminent death is a desire to climb Machu Picchu, learn to fly airplanes, and visit every baseball stadium in the United States, rather than do what a responsible adult with a family would and should do if he found out he had precious months to live, such as plan for his family's future without him, spend his last days with his children, and as he says, "use his few remaining months to make this planet a better place than the way he found it." What Queenan is actually describing is the kind of self-focused parenting that many emerging adults have been raised with. Humor may be his conduit, but the lesson of this kind of parenting is clear. Immaturity begets immaturity, and the research bears this out.

The New Media Generation

Baby boomers and Gen Xers grew up with television. Yet despite their fluency in all things media, they can't hold a candle to the current generation of young people. Professor Jane Brown from the University of North Carolina at Chapel Hill says that, culturally and developmentally, emerging adults growing up in the early part of the twenty-first century are unlike any others in history. The media has an unrelenting presence in their daily lives, so much so that Brown refers to them as "the new media generation."

Emerging adults turn to television not only for entertainment but also as a source of information, and according to researcher

Get real. Anyone contemplating an attempt at being a star needs to be very honest with him- or herself about his or her true talents and assets. For any would-be stars, getting some professional opinions rather than going exclusively on the fact that your friends, mom, and dad all keep telling you that you're gonna be a big star, should be the first step.

Moms and dads: I'm not for a minute suggesting that you stop being supportive of your kids. What I am suggesting is that you do your best to help your children develop genuine self-esteem based on substantial personal qualities, skills, and talents. Also, make sure they are represented by professionals who know their industry, rather than relying on the untried opinions of the people who love them.

L. Monique Ward, this has lead them to have a greater level of involvement with the content they view. They don't merely watch TV. They feel TV. They live TV. What they see on television reflects their world or—in the case of reality television—it *is* their world.

There is an abundance of reality shows that feature young people striving to become America's next top singer, dancer, model, or soap star; vying to be selected as the fairy tale husband or wife for a fairy tale hunk or hunkette; out-surviving one another in a jungle or on a menacing, remote island; attempting to stay sane while held captive under twenty-four-hour surveillance, with apparently little more than a swimsuit and some lip gloss; or simply struggling to get through the dramas of young life and love in a suitably stunning beachside location.

So, emerging adults spend a lot of time watching their peers on TV, peers doing (relatively) normal, everyday things that *they* could do just as well—no, better. All their peers had to do to get on TV was send in audition tapes that captured the TV producers' attention. In many cases the stars of reality TV have no discernible talent, just good looks. Now they're celebrities . . . for a while at least. And this persuades emerging adults that celebrity is not only desirable, but it's within their reach.

Casting director Olivia Harris confirms that there has been a change in the industry, away from talent toward youth and good looks. Even for dramatic roles, actors regularly show up cute, yet unprepared, something that would never have happened twenty years ago. "Your chances of getting a job are a lot greater [if you are beautiful], since there are so many shows demanding pretty young people," she says. Another big change she has seen over the years is that "now they walk in and say, 'I want to be famous,'" whereas in the past "even if you were thinking it you wouldn't *say* it."

Paris Hilton is my favorite example of this era of kids, and I have been on *Showbiz Tonight* and the Fox News Channel many times saying that she is the "hood ornament" for this generation, their icon. Famous for being famous, she seems to have it all—money, celebrity, power, looks, glamour—without having to really *do* anything. Despite the fact that they don't have the riches, opportunity, or upbringing that she has had, many emerging adults harbor fantasies of enjoying the same lifestyle as her. And with it all looking so easy on TV, and parents saying, "Yes, you are special," it's no wonder it seems attainable.

Reality TV is making celebrities out of people who should not be, and it's encouraging others to follow in their footsteps. We are raising a generation of kids who think they're special, therefore we *should* want to watch their every boring humdrum move. Despite the fact that MTV ran out of interesting people on *The Real World* after season four, they trudge on. So far they've shot twenty seasons, and I'm sure there is no shortage of kids lining up to audition for seasons twenty-one, twenty-two, and twenty-three.

Reality TV is making celebrities out of people who should not be, and it's encouraging others to follow in their footsteps.

Reality Check

While the lure of fame is tempting, and it may look easy to achieve, members of the new media generation need to consider a few things before they give up their day jobs or trade college for singing lessons.

Of all the reality-show stars churned out each year, most never actually go on to "make it" by true success standards, nor do they become enduringly famous. Maybe they do for just a few seconds, or for their "15 minutes," as Andy Warhol predicted. (Although I've read that

Keep your bases covered. Even teenagers who are brilliantly gifted at something—music, acting, a sport—need a well-rounded education. If the going gets tough, they will need solid skills to fall back on. Peter Scales, Ph.D., of the Search Institute, a nonprofit organization devoted to the raising of healthy children and youth, warns talented young sportspeople not to fall for what he calls the "NBA fallacy." Only 1 in 10,000 kids actually has enough talent to compete at the college level, and then 1 in every 100,000 of them actually makes it into the pros. "The odds are astronomically against them, but a lot of young people want to be NBA stars. They figure, 'I don't have to worry about English or math, I'll let my agent deal with all of that.' They can't string an actual grammatical sentence together and, worse, some brag about their lack of education."

as a celebrity himself Warhol got so sick of commenting on that famous quote that he changed it each time he was asked about it: "In the future, fifteen people will be famous," or "In the future, everyone will be famous to fifteen people," which is probably true if you consider the blogosphere and YouTube.) I can list a litany of names that were everywhere and have now sunk back into obscurity. Colleen Haskell—who? Dat Phan—huh? Yeah, that's the point.

Many of the agents, producers, and casting people whom I spoke with were very clear that only the most talented of reality-TV stars are likely to continue to find work in the entertainment industry. As an agent for TV show hosts, Mark Turner of the Abrams Artists Agency sees former reality-TV stars almost daily. "Over the past ten years, I've had more and more people who've been contestants or participants on reality shows contact me looking to turn what they've done into a full-time TV career. While some have been fortunate enough to make the difficult transition, I've found that it's far and away the exception, rather than the rule." Anyone who hopes to follow the lead of Elizabeth Hasselbeck—former *Survivor* contestant, now panelist on *The View*—is likely to be sorely disappointed, as she is a rarity.

Maroulis cautions: "It's a marathon, not a sprint. There are people wondering what happened to me [after *American Idol*], but if they even knew how hard I've worked and about my family and the struggles . . . I had a giant sitcom deal lined up right after *AI*, starring Kelsey Grammer. I spent that vital year right after *AI* doing that show." But as so often happens in TV land, the network canned the show before it made it on air. "But I have big shoulders . . . I've always been a survivor. I always hustle. Even as a kid, I always had jobs; I had more Mcjobs than anyone I know." Since *Idol* Maroulis has had a role on *The Bold and the Beautiful*, owns and runs his own record label (Sixth Place Records/Sony Red), and has released a self-titled album.

A few minutes of fame might be relatively easy to snatch, but forging an entire career based on that quick fame is hard to do. Ereka Vetrini, who was a contestant on the first season of *The Apprentice*, is a great example of the struggle a reality-show contestant can have making the transition to working TV host. After *The Apprentice*, Vetrini went on to work as Tony Danza's sidekick for the first season of *The Tony Danza Show*. By the second season she was gone, literally replaced by a parrot—and the rumors began to fly.

Speculation about the reason Vetrini was fired varied from her lack of experience and ability to the opposite, that she was so camera friendly and likeable that Danza felt threatened by her. While in Chicago shooting the now defunct *In the Loop with iVillage*, she explained to me, "My role was never fully defined [on *The Tony Danza Show*] and proved not to fit in with the formula of the show, but in just one season I learned so much." I asked if she felt prepared to go from a network reality show to a network talk show. "Absolutely not. I had no idea what I was in for, and in retrospect that was a good thing . . . I think what the executive producers liked about me was that I was not overtrained." *The Tony Danza Show* was canceled after the second season.

So what is it like to be an instant celebrity because of a reality show? Vetrini says that while she did become a celebrity "of sorts," it wasn't all that you would imagine. "For a while I made the most of it. I went to the parties, got the VIP treatment, and walked the red carpet, but I remember feeling like a phony. What was I 'famous' for?"

After it all faded—as it always does—she remembered who she was and where she came from and realized, "I take pride in working hard and being good at what I do. I was not good at being famous just for being famous."

Reality-show contestants and reality shows in general are the bane of an actor's existence and certainly of writers, film directors, and casting directors. These people worked very hard to get where they are, honed their crafts, and worked as gofers, extras, and assistants, getting coffee for the people whose jobs they so desperately wanted. True artists know the feeling of rejection, a hard day's work, and how long real success can take. So of course they resent reality stars, because they just show up. Imagine if you went to work tomorrow and someone walked in off the street with absolutely no experience and replaced you? You wouldn't like it much either. Harris told me: "I actually got a call once to cast [a reality show]. It's *anti* casting! I said, 'What is there to cast? Just open the door.'"

According to the Screen Actors Guild (SAG), acting roles are disappearing at an alarming rate. In 2005, for the second year in a row, theatrical and television employment statistics took a downward turn, due to the major networks adding yet another 5.1 hours per week of nonscripted (read: reality show) programming. The latest casting data released by SAG put the number of roles for performers, especially in the field of prime-time television, at an all-time low.

Millions of young people want to be actors, but only 120,000 even get into SAG. And of that number, very few—only about fifty—might be considered stars. We've all heard of big-name stars earning notoriously huge salaries, such as Kiefer Sutherland, who signed on to do *24* for a reported $40 million. This creates the false impression that acting is a highly paid job, but according to the U.S. Department of Labor, the median hourly rate for actors is $11.28. The average income that a SAG member earns from acting? Less than $5,000 a year.

Beyond the fact that for most chasing a career in the entertainment industry is a wasted effort, it's also important to remember that even if you do manage to grasp fame, it doesn't necessarily equal happiness.

Singer-songwriter Edwin McCain has some insight—he lived it: "I went through years where I thought my [expletive] didn't stink, and I became the worst version of myself. I traveled in a private jet, had limo drivers, and acted like a complete idiot. I guarantee if you were with me then, you were having a good ole' time. But fame robs pieces of your soul that you are never getting back, and self-respect goes out the window. It's irretrievable." McCain now chooses not to live in Hollywood or New York. He lives in the town where he was born—Greenville, South Carolina—because, he says, "At the end of the day, you are still a friend to your friends and a son to your parents."

"Fame robs pieces of your soul that you are never getting back."

—EDWIN MCCAIN

Celebrity should be the result, not the goal. It's time for emerging adults to focus on developing skills and useful personal traits instead of just chasing the fame ideal. McCain advises, "There's a certain amount of trial by fire, and while I welcome all comers, the incinerator is 220 degrees and they'll get burned up. Only the ones who are Teflon coated will survive."

Strengthen your core. I'm not talking abs. I mean that we all need to focus on the personal qualities that really matter, that really endure, such as competency, compassion, empathy, social skills, and solid self-esteem. These things, much more than the fleeting joys of fame, are what are important. Once the sparkle has faded, what really matters is a strong sense of self and your place in your family and community.

CHAPTER FIVE

It's Not a Generation Gap, It's a Freakin' Ravine

I think young girls look up to people who are older than they are, because you're always looking ahead.

AMANDA BYNES, QUOTED IN *USA TODAY,* AUGUST 15, 2005

Since the dawn of time, community elders have been shocked by the behavior of the young. Way back in 400 B.C., Socrates famously carped, "The children now love luxury; they have bad manners, contempt for authority; they show disrespect for elders, and love chatter in place of exercise." (What did he know? Pilates, yoga, personal trainers, and gym memberships are at an all-time high.) That statement could have been made at any time in history to illustrate how the older generation looks at the next one, shaking their heads in despair of what the future holds. Down through the millennia it has always been the role of the younger generation to take their lives in a radically different direction than their parents'.

In living memory it's the baby boomers who raised Cain in a truly significant way. They outraged their parents with social statements and antiwar protests. They forced society to change its attitudes on marriage, women's rights, and race. All in all they shook the very foundations of society. Some of the younger baby boomers and subsequent Gen-X parents are worried—not that their children will become antiestablishment rebels like the boomers, but the opposite. They're concerned their daughters might conform to the worst of standards and end up like Paris Hilton, Lindsay Lohan, or Britney Spears, with goals that don't go much further than getting off a charge for a traffic violation or buying the latest Chanel bag. They hope their sons will aspire to more than a life of bling, luxury cars, Cristal, and a regular supply of whatever the latest class-A drug is.

Even young celebrities are worried about their children developing the habits of other young celebrities. On my radio show I interviewed Kevin Federline, at the time still Britney Spears's husband, and the father of her two sons. Their firstborn, only a year old, was already showing talent, Federline told me. "It's funny, I watch Preston doing his thing to a beat and really having rhythm." Stage moms and dads all over the country were dyspeptic with envy, but through his then bride Federline knew enough about the world of celebrity to be cautious. "I don't plan on letting any of my kids be in the industry until they are eighteen and ready to make decisions like that for themselves. . . . I'm the dad that doesn't want to put my kids out there. Y'know, I think child stars grow up with a lot of problems. I'm gonna avoid that as much as possible."

"I think child stars grow up with a lot of problems."

—KEVIN FEDERLINE

Just about every day it seems that a celebrity commits some new outrage against human decency. I don't know how anyone is brave enough to drive in LA— aren't the roads filled with drunk-driving and/or drug-addled starlets? If you're not seeing a star's wasted-looking mug shot on your TV screen, you're hearing about the latest leaked nude photo or sex tape. Talk shows, newspapers, magazines, and blogs are alive with debate about what kind of damage these role models are doing to the young people who idolize them.

It is *young girls* that parents seem to be the most worried about when it comes to these celebrity role models. No doubt this is because there is so much more airtime devoted to the antics of a certain clique of young female celebrities—the ones that little girls just happen to adore. While there are no doubt plenty of male stars getting into all kinds of trouble, and while we'd prefer our sons didn't follow in their footsteps either, they just don't seem to be under quite the same media microscope.

That's not to say boys are not influenced. Several studies have been published in the past few years that suggest male body-image issues are on the rise. But there doesn't seem to be such a glut of information about male celebrities.

This topic is so hot that I have been asked on to an increasing number of television shows to offer my opinion—from the developmental psychology point of view—about the effect the constant media exposure to stars' behavior is having on young girls. When Lindsay Lohan was arrested for DUI the second time, it was like DEFCON 1 at my place. Everyone wanted to know what this meant for her career, what kind of role model she was becoming, and what parents could do to protect their children from following in her footsteps. And when I say everyone, I mean not only programs such as *Showbiz Tonight* that cover celebrity news exclusively, but also news channels rarely known for lengthy discussions of celebrity culture like *The O'Reilly Factor* on the Fox News Channel. The stories would center not on the demise of a starlet's career, but on the effect it was having on the youth who admire her. Parents were indeed concerned, and understandably so.

Let's not forget that the youth have always pulled through, got jobs, set up their own homes, and raised their very own generation of youth.

Children of the Celebrity Age

Parenting is stressful enough. You want your children to have the best education possible so they can have a secure career. Then there are all those other concerns you are reminded of daily. What if they're being pressured into drugs, alcohol, or smoking by their friends? What about bullying, youth suicide, self-esteem?

And now should you have to add celebrity role models to your list?

Well, let's not forget our old friend Socrates and his version of, "Oye, kids today!" Keep in mind that every grown-up generation has despaired of the problems

Focus on positive celebrity role models. It may seem that all young female Hollywood does is drink, take drugs, and drive. They forget they had babies and think, "Yeah, great idea," everytime a boyfriend suggests turning on the video camera. But there are a host of young female stars leading lives of accomplishment and dignity—it's just that they're focusing on their education, career, family, and community, and that doesn't make such a juicy *Access Hollywood* story.

It seems as though our expectations of stars' behavior is directly proportional to the caliber of actor we perceive them to be. Could you picture Natalie Portman speeding away from the paparazzi after leaving a club at 4 a.m. and driving into oncoming traffic with Harrison Ford in the passenger seat? She is known for her consistency, talent, and integrity—not for showing up hours late to a film set still on a bender from the night before. There is a level of professionalism and respect some actors have for their profession that we all wish young Hollywood possessed.

You might not have much control over your kids' taste in entertainers, but next time you get palpitations when they're looking at pictures of bleary-eyed starlets hobbling out of a limo at a nightclub, it might help to remember girls such as Natalie Portman, Mandy Moore, Claire Danes, Rachel McAdams, Rosario Dawson, and America Ferrera, among others.

besetting their youth. And let's also not forget that the youth have always pulled through, got jobs, set up their own homes, and raised their very own generation of youth . . . to angst about. My mother was just as horrified when my friends and I were walking around dressed like Madonna, who back in the 1980s was the "Don't be like her" woman of the day. We turned out okay.

We are so inundated with different forms of media and technology bringing celebrity images into our lives that it's easy to get overwhelmed. And because we may be overwhelmed, it's natural to assume that children and teens are, too. We fear that they will be unable to sift through all the media images of celebrities, edit out the "noise," and absorb the right kind of messages.

But let's put this into perspective. I'll bet that you had to deal with a lot more technology, bringing many more media images into your life, than your own mother did. As the pace of technological change speeds up, each previous generation inevitably feels overwhelmed or out of touch. Take my grandmother, who still doesn't understand the answering machine. She still—to this day—calls and leaves the following message: "Tell her it's Grandma," like I'm going to come home and a robot of some kind will tap me on the shoulder and say, "Good day, madam, I'm sorry to disturb you, but I just wanted to inform you that your grandmother has telephoned." Or sometimes she will say her piece and then sign it, "Love always, Grandma," like it's teletyping my messages to me. "This just in—STOP—Grandma has called—STOP." She has the voicemail feature on her phone but doesn't know how to use it, so when you call her and she isn't home, it just rings and rings. We could teach her what to do, but since she didn't grow up with any of this kind of technology, she doesn't really understand what she's missing—other than calls from her doting . . . make that *frustrated* . . . grandchildren. To her, technology was a typewriter, which was a very big deal (although she never learned to use that, either).

To my grandmother it seems impossible, or at least improbable, that we are actually capable of using the kinds of communication we have today. When she was twenty-two and the guy she was dating wanted to dump her, he had to do it in person and not over (choke) e-mail. When she got to know a guy, she went to places that young grandmas and their gentlemen callers went to, talked face-to-face, and shared a milkshake or whatever they drank back then.

My point is, the way her generation, and even our parents' generation, process information is different from the way we do. And yep, that means the ability of the current crop of children and teens to process information—editing and weeding out what is not relevant—is evolving at a faster rate than we perhaps give them credit for. These are the babies of the information technology age; an endless stream of media images of celebrities is what they were born into, and we need to recognize that they, too, just as other generations have done before them, are constantly adapting and learning how to process all this information and imagery. Just

These are the babies of the information technology age; an endless stream of media images of celebrities is what they were born into.

as you have no trouble leaving an answering machine message for someone, your kids are probably doing a better job of editing down the flood of celebrity information than you realize.

Children are becoming comfortable with technology at younger and younger ages. When I was doing my practicum at Nickelodeon for grad school, I worked on a study that found that kids as young as two and three years old were able to turn on a computer and click on their icon on the desktop. Maybe they couldn't read yet, but they knew how to work the computer and what their icon looked like. This speaks to not just the ease with which technology makes its way into each generation, but how young people learn to adapt. Part of being able to adapt is making technology fit into your life and not the other way around. But when children at any age participate in normal social developmental stuff such as e-mailing, watching entertainment TV, and reading celebrity blogs, it seems to parents as if it's just *everywhere* and that kids must be absorbing more than they can handle.

The fact that celebrities are all pervasive doesn't necessarily mean that they are all-powerful, though. Sure, kids today may be exposed to the most extreme volume of images of celebrities that anyone up to this point in human history has been, but is this endless stream of celebrity images turning them all into drunk drivers? Cocaine addicts? Pole dancers? Happily, no.

Parent vs. Celebrity Death Match

You may be relieved to hear that the likelihood of your child ending up with self-esteem problems, aggression, a drug or alcohol addiction, or a jail term has little to do with the celebrity images he or she is exposed to every day. Youth have had their troubles for as long as there have been youth—way, way before MTV hit the airwaves—before there even *were* airwaves. But don't put your feet up just yet. The stars might be largely off the hook, but that leaves the onus on us, the grown-ups at home, to be ever more vigilant.

In the past twenty years or so, the trend has been to blame kids' problems—everything from violent behavior to poor self-image, learning and concentration problems, and narcissism—on too much exposure to TV, the Internet, movies, and video games. And a major component of what kids see in the media is celebrity images. James Steyer, who teaches civil rights and civil liberties at Stanford University, is an advocate for children. On CNN one day he said, "The average American child today spends approximately forty hours per week with various forms of media—television, music, video games, films. Maybe about seventeen hours per week with their parents, and about thirty hours per week in school. So you tell me, who's the parent in this picture?" Well, Jim, the parent. The parent is still the parent. That's something we all have to remember: Parents have the final say over what their kids do and what they watch. Anyone who leaves the parenting to video games, TV, and the Internet has only him- or herself to blame.

Peter Scales, Ph.D., is a developmental psychologist, author, speaker, and researcher who is widely recognized as one of the nation's foremost authorities on children, youth, and families. He agrees that the parent is still responsible for teaching children constructive use of their time, values, and social competencies. He has a theory about why celebrities don't make great role models: "If kids are trying to imitate people whose lives are not about authenticity, where all we know about them is superficiality and appearances, where they are playing a role for the camera, there is no humility or giving to others there.

"Celebrity worship, in its worst manifestations, is counterproductive. The right kinds of positive values can have an impact on an adolescent's identity, but if the culture of celebrity . . . [is about the stars] promoting themselves [and] high self-esteem is demonstrated on a superficial level, it's not the right kind of positive impact.

"What Britney and Lindsay actually signify are behaviors that are not evidence of high self-esteem but a shallow idea of what it looks like. Acting as if the world revolves around you may come across as high self-esteem, but it is completely superficial."

"What Britney and Lindsay actually signify are behaviors that are not evidence of high self-esteem but a shallow idea of what it looks like."

—PETER SCALES, PH.D.

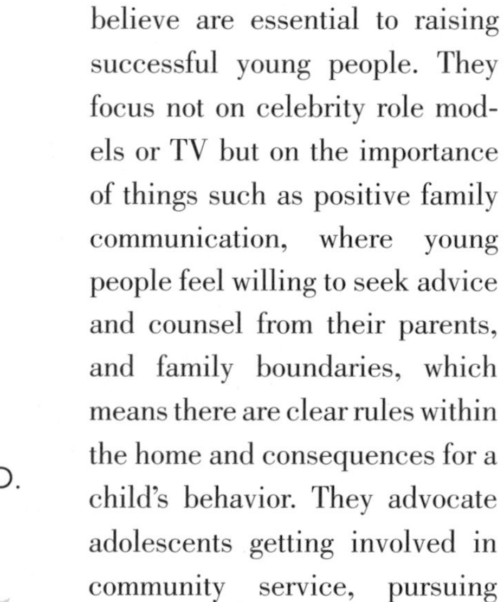

Scales and Peter Benson, Ph.D., through their Search Institute facility, have come up with 40 Developmental Assets for Adolescents™, which are the positive experiences and qualities they believe are essential to raising successful young people. They focus not on celebrity role models or TV but on the importance of things such as positive family communication, where young people feel willing to seek advice and counsel from their parents, and family boundaries, which means there are clear rules within the home and consequences for a child's behavior. They advocate adolescents getting involved in community service, pursuing creative endeavors, and having convictions.

Communicate positively. If you have concerns about how your children are being influenced by the media and celebrity culture, Scales advises that you "talk with your children about your fears and concerns, but expect an amount of good decision making on their part and reward it." This is a way to keep them close. Remember: "It's trial and error to be a teen, and trial and error to be a parent of a teen. You have to always give them the opportunity to reject you, but keep inviting them to be with you, while expecting to hear 'No.'" You need to expect a certain amount of rejection, because "that's the process; that's how it works."

Set family boundaries. Setting boundaries is about being as consistent as possible with rules, but understanding that as your child's needs change, the rules and boundaries need to change as well. Scales suggests: "Lessen the parental reins sooner on clothing and music but continue to have the family computer in a family room with parental filters on it." Parental monitoring "has to get negotiated, and your child tells you at what age that starts, just as they tell you when it's time [you] stop accompanying them to the restroom." In terms of how strict you should be with your children, Scales believes that "extremes are not good at either end. It's not good to be too permissive and trying to be their friend—they don't want you or need you as a friend, they need you as a parent. Authoritarian parenting leads to fear, which is not a good long-term motivator. What you have to do is, you have to be loving."

Scales notes that parents and the media often discuss the negative influence of celebrity and pop culture on adolescents, and he is keen to put the issue in perspective. "There is probably a subgroup who are more vulnerable, but it's a distinct minority. The majority are quite close to their parents, they are not doing poorly at school." Nor, he adds, is the majority engaging in the worst kinds of celebrity behavior. Scales points out that teen pregnancy and teen smoking rates are down, and teenagers are the most likely to volunteer their time to charities and community groups. For the most part parents need not worry that their kids are copying trashy young celebrities.

In 2007 I was on *The Star Jones Show* on the former Court TV discussing the main influences and role models for teen girls. "I can see that it is harder than it used to be to get through adolescence today," Star said, "especially as it seems that young girls have very few young role models that . . . the media elevates for them to emulate." And she was100 percent right.

But fortunately most girls turn elsewhere for their role models. I shared with the panel that day a study that I had conducted a few years back, in which I interviewed 238 girls between the ages of thirteen and twenty-four asking, among other questions, who their role models were. The largest percentage, over 70 percent of the girls polled, said that their role model was a parent or an older sister. Very few chose a celebrity; one or two chose a political figure. Star agreed and said that she, too, felt that her main role model was indeed her mother. These findings speak to how influential a parent, or an older sibling, can be in a girl's life.

You are the role model. No matter how much time children spend absorbing media images of celebrities, their role model will always be their mother, sister, or other close female guardian. And that means they will model their behavior on yours. Be careful that you're not saying one thing to children—"You don't need to be skinny and perfect-looking like those stars"—but then actually doing another, such as going on crash diets, working out to excess, and toying with the idea of plastic surgery.

The Kurt Cobain Effect

Perhaps the ultimate nightmare scenario for any parent is that their child might become so depressed, isolated, or troubled that they take their own life. And when a celebrity who happens to be an idol for young people does just that, we all fear the copycat suicides of their young fans. It just seems to make sense that if someone kids look up to takes a certain course of action, it gives it credence and validity. As so often in life, though, what seems like an obvious conclusion to draw might not be so obvious after all.

Some researchers, such as psychologist David Phillips, claim to have found links between highly publicized suicides and increases in the suicide rate— but there is just as much evidence that contradicts this theory. A prime example is the suicide of rock idol Kurt Cobain in April 1994.

Lead singer of the Seattle band Nirvana, Cobain's music spoke to the anger that many of his generation felt. As one of the authors of the grunge movement, he was embraced by millions of Gen Xers who felt that the preceding generation, the boomers, had partied for thirty years and left them with the bill. Cobain's lyrics, presence, and supernova stardom deeply touched an entire generation of teens and young adults like no one else's had in quite some time. His truth was their truth. He was not supposed to commit suicide; he was supposed to continue to be a prolific artist and an iconoclast to be admired. The story of his dramatic death, from a self-inflicted gunshot wound to the head, was told in unprecedented detail in newspapers and on TV, complete with photographs of the gruesome scene.

Would his suicide, and the media coverage of it, have a negative influence on depressed, suicidal teenagers who identified with their fallen hero? Researchers Graham Martin and Lisa Koo decided to find out, and they published a study in the *Archives of Suicide Research* in 1997. Teen suicides had dropped between 1981 and 1984, according to the *American Journal of Psychiatry*. Martin and Koo wanted to know: Would the Cobain suicide coverage undo all of that, just a decade later?

Seattle crisis clinics received an increased number of phone calls for counseling after the news of Cobain's suicide broke. Talking about your feelings in these situations is helpful, so that was good. However, in the thirty days following Cobain's death, there were six suicide deaths of young people by gunshot wounds to the head. That sounds grim, I know, but what that figure actually represented was a marked *decrease* in suicides compared to the rate during the previous five years. The researchers concluded that Cobain's suicide had *not* encouraged young people to take their lives (but that those who did take their lives were statistically destined to do so but may have been influenced to use the same method he did).

Clearly this celebrity's action had affected his young followers—just not exactly the way everybody expected it to. So why did the suicide of a rock icon, particularly one who projected an anti-establishment ethos, fail to inspire his vulnerable population of fans to do the same? The researchers offered a couple of possible explanations: Many of Cobain's fans learned of his death through music Web sites and entertainment news reports that speculated the death to be a murder, and many believed that theory. But perhaps most interesting, the researchers made a link to the way his widow, Courtney Love, responded to his suicide: publicly condemning his actions and repeatedly referring to him in foul language. She read aloud his suicide note and shocked his fans with her honesty, perhaps helping them to understand the anguish suicide causes to the ones left behind. No matter how you feel about Love, she may have saved lives that day by opening up to the fans. Celebrities can use their powers for good.

No matter how you feel about Courtney Love, she may have saved lives that day by opening up to the fans. Celebrities can use their powers for good.

Other researchers have speculated that Cobain's death may have made the public more sensitive to youth suicide, prompting parents, teachers, and friends to take extra care with those they felt might have been at risk.

All of this reminds us that hiding things from people is worse than telling the painful truth; and danger lies in the unspoken rather than in the spoken. It makes Dr. Scales' point all the more relevant, that what families really need is positive communication.

Lollipop Land

Who among us has not gasped in horror at the sight of a formerly healthy-looking star on the red carpet now looking too thin, with shoulder blades jutting out like dangerous weapons and a lollipop head that's way too big for her body? Angelina Jolie, Renée Zellweger, Teri Hatcher, the Olsen twins, Nicole Richie, Keira Knightley, Kate Bosworth. The list of famous women who have been cited for their dramatic weight loss goes on and on.

Eating disorders such as anorexia and bulimia, and the trend among girls to begin dieting at younger ages, cause as much anxiety among parents as the obesity epidemic. And when girls are bombarded daily—if not hourly—with media images of thin and gorgeous female stars, it leaves many parents wondering whether it may push their daughters toward poor body image and eventually an eating disorder. A group of mothers I interviewed for this book had daughters in the same dance school, and one of the moms had this to say, "We don't put any pressure on her to look a certain way, nor do we even discuss weight at home, yet I wonder why my daughter, who doesn't have a weight problem at all, is always dieting. She's a dancer, so is it the girls in her dance class who are sending her this message, or are the body image problems due to celebrities who are thin?"

Celebrity Beauty Fest

That we are surrounded by images of beautiful celebrities in the media is nothing new. Every generation has had its beauties. Perhaps one of the most iconic, and the woman who immediately springs to mind, is Marilyn Monroe. There is only one Marilyn. But if they'd had the Internet and cable TV in her day, would she have been quite so unique? Might there have been a profusion of Marilyn-like stars, their images swamping TV screens and inboxes on a daily basis? In the 1980s, for the Gen Xers, being beautiful was mainly for models, less so for musicians, TV stars, and the like. In the 1960s and 1970s, there were exceptional female stars who stood out for their beauty, such as Raquel Welch, Ali McGraw, or Barbara Bach—but every female celebrity didn't have to look like them.

From the 1990s onward, it has become increasingly apparent that entertainers—be they actors, TV anchors, or singers—have to look a certain way in order to find work. If you don't think so, ask casting director Olivia Harris, whose job it is to cast young actors for television. She tells me, "Now [casting breakdowns] all say: 'Susie, 21, gorgeous. Fred, 21, gorgeous' . . . you perpetuate this culture where everybody is gorgeous!" *That* is new.

It's the same in the music industry. Before the advent of music videos thirty or so years ago, singers didn't *have* to be physically attractive. Darryll Brooks (who has worked with Prince, Stevie Wonder, and Mya, among others) says, "Physical appearance, sex appeal, and charisma have always mattered, it's just that we are now in a visual world with videos, promotion, and marketing. Back in the day, the album cover was the only chance you had."

Many blame celebrities, models, and the media for eating disorders, but that should only be one part of a wider discussion. The causes of eating disorders are complex and many. According to a 2006 study in the *Archives of General Psychiatry*, genetics accounts for 56 percent of all eating disorders. Everything from child abuse, depression, and feeling a lack of control, to the search for unhealthy perfectionism, have been implicated as well.

And when it comes to body image—and a girl's self-esteem as a whole—once again, it turns out parents play a crucial role. Some parents prime their daughters with the idea that their looks are the most important thing. They comment constantly on their daughters' hair, clothes, or weight—either criticizing or praising. And while they may think they're helping them to learn to take care of themselves and their appearance, these parents may be doing more harm than they realize. The danger is that they may create kids who view their perfect appearance as vital to their parents' love and attention, and they begin to see it as a valuable currency. These girls learn to associate being thin and perfect looking with being loved and happy—the things that all human beings want. For vulnerable girls like this, there is the potential that images of what seem like perfect celebrity bodies could reinforce their own desperation for the perfect body.

On the other hand, parents who praise their children for more substantial qualities, such as how smart they are, what a great friend they are, or how hard they work, provide the ideal antidote to the images of starved celebrity glamour. A girl who has a strong overall sense of self-esteem is more likely to look at a picture of a beautiful, thin star such as Kate Hudson and say to herself, "That's her, this is me, so what?" rather than use the star as a yardstick for how she is supposed to look.

Clinical psychologist and eating disorder specialist Kimberly Lawrence Kol, Psy.D., believes that eating disorders can be tied to celebrity worship in the following way: "When girls are constantly presented with perfect bodies that receive love, admiration, glamour, success, and power, there is a risk they will start to believe that having that perfect body is the only way to get all those desirable things."

"When girls are constantly presented with perfect bodies that receive love, admiration, glamour, success, and power, there is a risk they will start to believe that having that perfect body is the only way to get all those desirable things."

—KIMBERLY LAWRENCE KOL, PSY.D.

Kol suggests that parents talk to their kids "about everything . . . not just drugs and sex, but also the media and how it impacts us unless we are careful. It's our job to help our kids understand how and why they are being influenced, how to withstand it, and which parts are potentially dangerous and which parts are okay. . . . You have to prepare your kids."

It all comes down to helping your daughter build good self-esteem based on a solid foundation. "Anorexia, weight obsession, and body disturbance are fundamentally about not knowing oneself," Kol says. "So if I don't know who I am, how I'm supposed to be, or how to take care of myself, then I'll be searching for the answers outside myself and more prone to believe what I'm told by the media."

Help your child learn who she is. This is the key to it all. As soon as your daughter knows herself, she is less likely to be vulnerable to looking at celebrity images in the media and thinking that is who she needs to be in order to be accepted, loved, or successful. Get her on the right track early by helping her to develop self-esteem based on a solid foundation. Body image is only one piece of the puzzle. All the research on adolescent self-esteem suggests that it is complex and is made up of many elements: How a girl feels about not just her body but also the quality of her friendships, how competent she feels at school or in her job, how much empathy she possesses, and how good her overall life skills are.

CHAPTER SIX

I Bought It Because Jessica Simpson Said I Should

I don't use my "celebrity" to make a living. I don't do ads for suits in Spain like George Clooney, or cigarettes in Japan like Harrison Ford . . . . It's a complete contradiction of the social contract you have with your audience. I mean, Robert De Niro's advertising American Express.

RUSSELL CROWE, FROM AN INTERVIEW IN *GQ*

When I take my dog, whose name is Mr. Dog (don't ask), for a walk, he likes to sniff everything thoroughly, even though yesterday he sniffed the same tree, the same newspaper kiosk, the same trash can. My husband and I have decided that's how he catches up on his neighborhood news—it's his daily celebrity jones. We don't know exactly what reports he is getting or how his gathering of doggie data helps him make decisions—in fact, what goes on inside his head is a mystery to us. He's smart and loving, yet he'll think nothing of cleaning himself in front of guests; he has a great sense of smell, yet he sometimes growls at his own reflection. Why? Because he has no self-awareness.

Not like you. As a human, you have a clear idea of who *you* are. You have the ability to make conscious decisions about what to do with your life, where to live, what to eat, what to wear, what to buy . . . don't you?

Before you start to feel too superior to Mr. Dog, consider this: Scientists still can't agree on where human consciousness and self-awareness even come from. The truth is, just as my dog relies on the aroma of a lamppost to decide which way he wants to walk each morning, you rely on a whole range of influences—your culture, society, family, peers, the media—to help form your consciousness. It's as if your parents went away for the weekend: No adult is in charge, anything goes, and from one moment to the next your choices can be influenced by the many varied messages you receive from the world around you. (If you could just sniff a lamppost to get your cues as to how you should behave, imagine how much simpler life would be!)

While this vulnerability may be news to you, it is something that advertisers and marketers know only too well and have been taking advantage of for many years in advertising, as well as in product placement in TV shows and movies. One of the key weapons in their arsenal is the celebrity endorsement. If we worship celebrities and aspire to their lifestyle, who better to influence our decisions; who better to tell us what we need to buy, who we need to be, which products and services we need to surround ourselves with? When a star makes a judgment from up high on their celebrity pedestal—I prefer *this* brand of cola, mascara, credit card, car insurance—it enters our consciousness, even though we may not be aware it's happening.

I don't think Mr. Dog was ever too concerned about what Eddie, the dog from *Frasier*, ate, and I don't think he's desperate to have the new cute outfit Jessica Simpson just put her dog, Daisy, in. But advertisers are banking on the fact that because Simpson is a celebrity, *I* will want to wear whatever she's wearing and buy whatever products she's endorsing. We are heavily

Celebrity-endorsed Childhood

If I had any doubts about whether spending habits are affected by celebrities, they vanished one night during my radio show when I had listeners call in to talk about the expensive things they'd bought their children. A divorced mom called to say that she purchased a $300 cell phone for her six-year-old daughter. The little girl had seen Hannah Montana star Miley Cyrus carrying one and begged her for it until she succumbed to guilt and bought it.

According to Teenage Research Unlimited, $53.8 billion is spent each year by families with children between three and twelve years old. The stakes get even higher when kids reach their teenage years. In 2006 alone, teenagers spent $189.7 billion, says a report by the market research company Packaged Facts, and it is predicted that figure will rise to $208.7 billion by 2011. And what are children and teens consuming? Anything a celebrity tells them to. A study published by the *Journal of Marketing* in 2006 found that one of the key assets advertisers have when they market to your children is . . . the celebrity endorsement. The fastest-growing consumer group for celebrity-endorsed goods is indeed teenagers.

influenced by celebrity culture, so it's no wonder that everywhere we turn there's a celebrity telling us what to buy.

The Human Brand

Most market researchers agree that celebrity is a powerful selling tool—not only for teens and children but for consumers of all ages. Advertisers aim to make a psychological connection between the product and a celebrity, to create what is called a "human brand." According to a study published by the American Marketing Association in 2006, we have a very strong attachment to human brands because early in life we learn to attach ourselves to humans. It is deeply embedded in us that human faces elicit emotional responses.

We are heavily influenced by celebrity culture, so it's no wonder that everywhere we turn there's a celebrity telling us what to buy.

We also learn to attend to the wants of other humans whom we trust, listen to what they tell us, and trust that what they say is true. As we grow, the same psychological process causes us to generalize to trusting celebrities when they tell us that we should buy brand A over brand B. Some research has also shown that a celebrity-endorsed product has a higher product recall rate, meaning you tend to remember a product in an ad better when a celebrity has lent his or her face and name to it.

Thanks to researchers Richard Petty and John Cacioppo, we know more about consumer psychology than ever before. They have a theory that says there are two ways we make up our minds about which products to buy. First, there is practical decision making based on diligent consideration and weighing the true merits of the available products. For example, you don't just buy a car based on how cute Lindsay Lohan looked crashing hers. You do some real investigation; you decide what your needs are, which car gets the best gas mileage, and which fits into your price range.

You tend to remember a product in an ad better when a celebrity has lent his or her face and name to it.

The second way we can choose a product is based on whether the product is associated with either a positive or a negative cue; that is, whether it gives us a good or a bad feeling. In this situation, you may buy a particular lipstick because you like the celebrity who endorses it or because it looks cute on Kelly Ripa. It is this second type of decision making that companies bank on—literally—when they hire a popular celebrity to be their spokesperson.

Take control. It's easy to be persuaded by celebrities, but when faced with a barrage of them telling you what you need to buy, you can stop, think, and question whether you really do need to make a purchase. I'm not suggesting that you treat every shopping decision in the analytical, detailed way you would select a new car, but bringing a little bit of that way of thinking into your everyday shopping certainly can't hurt. Don't get swept up in a celebrity fantasy and buy things you don't need . . . or worse, can't afford. Suze Orman always says, "We spend money we don't have to impress people we don't know or don't even like."

The Science of Celebrity Endorsement

According to Michael Kamins, Ph.D., of the University of Southern California, when a company chooses to use a celebrity in an advertisement, rather than an expert or an ordinary person, there is a science to choosing which celebrity to use. An ad agency must consider the celebrity's social risk: Is he married but rumored to be gay? Has she been divorced too many times? Is he a known drug addict? Another aspect to consider is the celebrity's level of exposure. Is this a celebrity who has too many endorsement deals that will conflict with the product or confuse the consumer? Or is it a celebrity who is already too much of a "brand"? Does she come with an image that is hard to change, an image that is larger than life—or in this case, larger than the product's image?

The demographic appropriateness of the star is crucial, too. In other words, who is it that the company is marketing to, and which celebrities do those people like? Shakira might be the perfect person if a company is selling a new lipstick to Latina women, but maybe she's not such a great choice for the Jazzy Power Chair.

Of course recognizability is vital. On a billboard you don't have time to explain that the guy holding the cola bottle played the guy who got killed in the second episode of *Heroes*, so it has to be someone who people can quickly identify. For a celebrity ad to work, you have to be able to look at it and immediately say, for instance, "Oh, that's Beyoncé in that [fill in the blank] ad—got it." And marketers want a celebrity who is attractive, likable, popular, and most important, honest.

Read the fine print. Should stars be trusted to give advice about financial products? I'm fairly certain they have someone who handles their investments, so they probably aren't the greatest experts on how to save for retirement. That guy from *Law & Order*, Sam Waterston, is a fine performer, but I doubt they taught him much about stock trading at acting school. Will you be any less up to your neck in debt because you have the same credit card as Robert De Niro and Ellen DeGeneres? Being persuaded by a star to buy a lipstick is not that big a deal, but being talked into the wrong financial product—or anything else with fine print, such as insurance or health care—certainly is.

The Rise of the Celebrity Designer . . . or, Kimora Lee Simmons Has Expensive Taste

Earlier I spoke of the Machine, that entity made up of production companies, agents, managers, and so on that creates celebrities. Now I'd like to add one more contributor to the list: *You*.

Stars such as Scarlett Johansson and Penelope Cruz seem to be making a significant amount of their income not from film salaries but from endorsement deals.

You create and nurture celebrity with your wallet. You help keep a star's career alive by consuming not only his or her movies, TV shows, or albums but also the products he or she advertises and endorses. Stars such as Scarlett Johansson and Penelope Cruz seem to be making a significant amount of their income not from film salaries but from endorsement deals.

Daniel Boorstin, credited as being the world's first social critic, has been quoted as saying, "A sign of celebrity is that his name is often worth more than his services." And how right he was, when you consider the explosion of clothing labels branded with celebrities' names. Lower-end department stores are aligning themselves with celebrity names daily, almost as if it's a race just to prove Boorstin's point.

It all began with Audrey Hepburn according to Dana Thomas, author of *Deluxe: How Luxury Lost Its Luster*. In her book she contends that the first celebrity-product alliance was between designer Hubert de Givenchy who, after dressing Hepburn for *Breakfast At Tiffany's* and *Charade*, "convinced her to pose for the advertising campaign for his perfume L'Interdit." In this day and age, the delicate, swanlike Audrey Hepburn might well have been lending her name to sweat pants or bed linens at Target. For that is the hold that celebrities now have on the marketing of products: It doesn't matter what your age group or income, there's a celebrity product for you. All of us are being asked to buy into a celebrity lifestyle.

In this day and age, the delicate, swan-like Audrey Hepburn might well have been lending her name to sweat pants or bed linens at Target.

But make no mistake, this doesn't mean we are living in a new age of equality with the stars. By way of illustration, let me tell you a little story about the shoes I wore to my wedding . . .

Those shoes were art. The moment I laid eyes on their heart-stopping splendor, I understood the power, sexiness, and utter opulence that men who flaunt expensive race cars or women who lavish themselves in sensational jewels

must feel. The shoes were five inches of silver Etain napa leather-covered spike heels with a glittering, bejeweled ankle strap. A second, entirely decorative, jewel-encrusted strap hung down as an ankle bracelet. It was by far the finest pair of shoes designer Manolo Blahnik had created. Although they cost almost as much as my gown, I did not hesitate to buy them. They were extraordinary, and I gave them their own bio in the wedding program.

A few weeks after my wedding, I saw a photograph of a casually dressed Kimora Lee Simmons coming out of a restaurant, or perhaps she was shopping for light bulbs—I forget exactly where she was or what she was doing, but it was something uneventful. I was less than delighted when I saw that she—on an ordinary day—was wearing my wedding shoes . . . with jeans, no less, as if they were ordinary shoes and not the precious works of art the I deemed them to be.

It was yet another reminder of how different stars are from the rest of us. With her popular Baby Phat and KLS fashion labels, the former high-fashion model and now reality-TV star and self-proclaimed "First Lady of Hip-Hop," has built a fashion empire based on what has been termed "the urban luxury movement." She sells us lower-end but glamorous-looking fashion, jewelry, cosmetics, and fragrances with her name on them—a pair of her strappy silver heels will set you back about $80. Meanwhile, though, *her* wardrobe is filled with Manolo Blahnik and designers so exclusive most of us wouldn't even recognize the names.

I don't begrudge the woman her luxury. If I had her wealth, I too would wear my wedding shoes to the grocery store. But what she is selling us is an image of wealth, taste, and high fashion and a message that says, "Yes, I know you cannot afford to live like I do, but here are some things you can afford that I completely approve of." To give credit where it's due, Simmons is regularly spotted at events wearing outfits from her own KLS line, but I doubt many other stars would wear their own label at a red-carpet event. It's one rule for them and another for us, despite the fact that it is our consumption of their products that affords them this lifestyle. Somehow it just doesn't seem right.

In Simmons's case, celebrity was her entree into establishing a successful fashion empire. Starting out as a Chanel model at the age of thirteen and later marrying hip-hop magnate Russell Simmons (the two are no longer together), she made the jump from celebrity to celebrity designer, a role that has fueled her iconic status. Thank goodness her clothes are as fabulous as she promised they would be.

It's one rule for them and another for us, despite the fact that it is our consumption of their products that affords them this lifestyle.

Most other successful designers start out as struggling young creative types, happy to simply have their clothes seen outside the workroom. Then one day, fashion and celebrity met. Retailers began to see the value of a designer's clothes when they were photographed on the personal-trainer-toned bodies of the Hollywood elite, launching unknown clothing engineers into highly sought-after fashion designers. The first question on the lips of red-carpet reporters is never about the movie being premiered or the star's nomination, it's "Who are you wearing?" This cements the reputations of a clique of exclusive designers whose clothes are worn by celebrities and coveted by the rest of us. It's no surprise, then, that budget fashion retailer H&M contracted Stella McCartney and Karl Lagerfeld to create a lower-end line to sell to us, or that Vera Wang designed a line for Kohls. But one of the first to expand his market from celebrity haute couture to suburban mall (and corresponding massive increase in turnover) may have been Isaac Mizrahi.

Mizrahi joined Target in 2002 to create an affordable version of his high-end couture clothing line. Clothes from his runway collections sell for thousands. One of my favorite dresses is a Mizrahi that I saw in a magazine, retailing for a mere eight grand, but at Target you could buy his pieces for $9.99 to $69.99. According to Target Corporation, from 2001 to 2007 the company's profits nearly quadrupled, which they partly attributed to the launch of high-profit clothing lines by Mizrahi and a slew of other celebrity designers who followed. It's not that we didn't shop at Target before, it's just that it wasn't as cool. Bringing in names such as Mizrahi gave the store the fashionista seal of approval. It's as if the clothes were blessed by the world of celebrity, like a rabbi deeming them, and thus Target, kosher.

Stealth Marketing

Sometimes it's not the overt sell, the "Look who we've got our Hanes on now," as much as the influence celebrities have when they are spotted carrying a certain handbag or wearing UGG boots. Stars can set off a consumer craze simply by being snapped with a product when they're out strolling with their baby or shopping with a girlfriend.

Paparazzi shots of celebrities such as Madonna and Oprah wearing Juicy Couture helped the company turn cute velour track pants into a multi-million-dollar business. There was no doubt stars loved hanging out in Beverly Hills in the comfy yet stylish gear, and Juicy Couture was able to capitalize on that. The design pair, Pam Skaist-Levy and Gela Taylor, didn't just hand out gift bags at awards ceremonies. Instead they might spend as much as $100,000 to take a suite in a five-star Hollywood hotel for a day, inviting celebrities and the all-important media to drop in and pick up samples of their latest line. Skaist-Levy and Taylor are smart ladies, because every time female stars such as Hilary Duff, Reese Witherspoon, Jessica Alba, Mischa Barton, or my Tori is snapped on the streets of LA or New York wearing Juicy, it's like free advertising for the label.

According to the Media Awareness Network, we are exposed to, on average, 3,000 ads per day. Advertising is becoming just white noise all around us and, especially since the advent of TiVo, it's becoming harder for advertisers to make us sit up and take notice of their products. So over the last decade or so, they have been using all sorts of new tricks—guerilla marketing, viral marketing, and product placement.

Starbucks has been said to indulge in this kind of marketing, but has it gone too far? In almost every celebrity weekly featuring Ben Affleck, Jennifer Garner, and their family, one of them, if not all, were seen carrying a venti Mocha Skim Latte Whatever. These pictures appeared so often that rumors began to fly that Starbucks had a seven-digit contract with the couple to be seen in public with their product, something the company and the actors' reps vehemently denied.

Before that it was the Olsen twins, who seemed to have Starbucks cups surgically attached to their lips at one point, and then it was Renée Zellweger. Those of you who get your caffeine fix from the popular chain are probably familiar with having your name scrawled on the side of the cup on a busy day, but do you walk down the street presenting your cup as if it were a nametag? I remember seeing one shot of Zellweger holding her Starbucks cup and in big black letters directly facing the camera, there was "Renée." Okay, it could have been a coincidence—but my point is, would you really blame a company for exploiting this not-so-subliminal effect?

Stars Behaving Badly

When an advertiser brings a celebrity onboard, it's a gamble in some regard. What if the celebrity gets caught doing something wrong, dragging the reputation of the product down with his or her own? This fear was given weight by the *Journal of the Academy of Marketing Science*, which warned marketers in 2006 that if a star behaves badly, consumers take it as a negative cue, fusing the star's tarnished image with the product he or she represents. Which is why every celebrity who gets involved in a scandal worries not only about his or her box office or album sales but about the income he or she will lose from advertising and endorsement deals. Companies pay millions to get the right celebrity, but many of their contracts stipulate that if the star behaves in a way that adversely affects the brand, the star can be dropped. You would think that would give stars an incentive to keep their noses clean, but that isn't always the case.

In one week in September 2007, Kiefer Sutherland made the news not once but twice, when it was announced that he was the only prime-time actor to make the *Forbes* list of top television earners, coming in at number twenty behind such notables as Oprah, who earned a reported $260 million, and David Letterman, with his measly $40 million. But only days before the list was published, Sutherland (which could work well as a single name—who else is named Kiefer?) had been caught making an illegal U-turn, failed a sobriety test, and was booked on yet another DUI, a charge that he had already pleaded "no contest" to back in 2004. But my concern was: Would Kiefer lose his Calorie Mate endorsement deal in Japan? How long could a company such as Calorie Mate stand behind this reckless behavior? Would the Japanese Mothers Against Drunk Driving (J-MADD) still buy Calorie Mate if it was endorsed by this rogue? Americans would never stand for such a thing, which may be why so many celebrities endorse products overseas. (Although in Kiefer's case, perhaps it was just as much to avoid the embarrassment of his fellow countrymen seeing him in the corniest of scenarios: as Jack Bauer saving the world from nuclear annihilation, one sip of energy-supplement drink at a time).

Celebrities having their endorsement deals pulled after big "oops" moments is nothing new. According to *Fortune* magazine, in an effort to get us back to the grill the beef industry hired actress Cybill Shepherd as a spokesperson in 1987, at the height of her popularity, but soon let her go when she publicly announced that she was a vegetarian. Also in the 1980s, Eric Clapton told *Rolling Stone* magazine that while his song "After Midnight" was being used in a Michelob Beer campaign, he was battling alcoholism in a detox facility.

While those are big oopsies and something the companies should have investigated thoroughly before shelling out millions of dollars, nothing is more absurd than Pepsi pulling Madonna's

1989 ad campaign because of the controversy that followed the airing of her "Like a Prayer" video. I say "absurd" because who did Pepsi think they were getting in bed with? Pat Boone? Marie Osmond? It was Madonna! She has made a career out of being a contrarian and creating controversy. It's what she's known for, and it's my guess that's why Pepsi wanted her in the first place. But when religious groups—inflamed by images in the video of burning crosses and Madonna bearing stigmata and getting intimate with a saint—threatened to boycott Pepsi products, her ads were pulled off the air and Pepsi canceled further campaigns she was contracted to do for the company.

Ironically they chose Britney Spears as one of their spokespeople in 2001, which was going well until she French-kissed Madonna on stage at the 2003 MTV Video Music Awards, a sort of passing of the Pepsi torch, or saliva, I suppose.

Michael Jordan had had his share of controversy, dogged by allegations that he was a compulsive gambler who racked up massive losses and promised to pay a former lover $5 million to stop her from going public about his adultery. Yet he continued to shill for McDonalds, Hanes, and Nike. Kobe Bryant, on the other hand, was let go from his McDonald's contract after being accused of rape, even though the case was dismissed when his accuser decided not to testify. It seems that Bryant had consensual sex outside of his marriage . . . which is, indeed, adultery. But prior to this accusation, Bryant was squeaky clean: a handsome man, an amazing athlete who spoke several languages, and the perfect role model. McDonald's dropped him, but not Jordan. I wonder what standards they used to make that decision.

For some brands—especially those that rely on a street-cred image—misbehavior can actually be seen as a plus. Supermodel

Kate Moss, rumored to have been a drug abuser, was nevertheless signed as a spokesperson by H&M, Chanel, and Burberry. Perhaps when the rumors remained simply that—rumors—they gave Moss a certain hip mystique the marketers thought was good for their brands. But when photographs of her nose deep in a few grams of cocaine were published in 2005, they acted surprised, canceled her contracts, and immediately distanced themselves from her. Cosmetics company Rimmel said they were "reviewing her contract" with them. It looked as though her career was finished.

But less than a year later, she had even more contracts than before, and her income was estimated to be *twice* what it was before the cocaine scandal. She had joined Audrey Hepburn and Jackie Kennedy in *Vanity Fair*'s Best Dressed Hall of Fame and was promoting Versace, Calvin Klein, Bulgari, Stella McCartney, UK cell phone company Virgin Mobile, and Nikon. She remained the face of Rimmel . . . and Burberry renewed her contract. Clearly these companies saw her not so much as a drug-addled mom potentially endangering her young daughter but more as someone whose dangerously chic image was just right for their brands. As

"Even a mantle of depravity can be worn with panache."

—AMY FINE COLLINS, *VANITY FAIR*, AUGUST 2006

Vanity Fair's Amy Fine Collins said in August 2006, "Even a mantle of depravity can be worn with panache."

The lesson here? While companies are often quick to express their outrage and disappointment over a celebrity's indiscretions, morals are a relative thing in the world of commerce. It seems that a celebrity's misbehavior is only considered bad when consumers threaten to stop buying the product he or she endorses.

What Halle Berry Knows About Makeup

Recently I was shopping at a cosmetics counter at a local high-end department store. Makeup artist Carmindy from TLC's *What Not To Wear* had been a guest on my radio show again and had suggested a particular eye pencil; I was there to see if I needed it (I did). I noticed a woman shopping next to me who had brought with her a page she had ripped out of a magazine, a Revlon ad featuring Halle Berry. Now, I don't need to remind you that Revlon isn't sold at high-end department stores, and as far as I know they do not have makeup counters, so I think this woman missed the point of the ad. Yet there she was rubbing each tester of eye shadow on the back of her hand and holding it up to the picture, trying to match Berry's color with the higher-end cosmetic. I could see the thought balloon over her head saying: "Revlon can't have better colors than this expensive brand, it *must* be here." She looked pensively at Berry, as if it were her fault.

Is it so surprising that she didn't trust the ad? As carried away as you might get by her alluring image, you know that a team of professionals put Halle together for that ad. Presumably they used Revlon products, but they also had the benefit of the best studio lighting, an army of makeup artists and stylists, an art director, one of the finest professional photographers in the business, and every celebrity's friend—someone skilled in the art of Photoshop to smooth out even the tiniest blemish or imperfection. And let's not forget, they had Berry's amazing face to use as a canvas. When you stop and think about it, you know that you aren't *really* going to look like Halle Berry if you buy that particular brand of eye shadow.

Perhaps there is no better illustration of the truth behind the celebrity-ad facade than Penelope Cruz's 2007 advertisements for a L'Oreal mascara that claimed to make eyelashes look 60 percent longer. The ad zoomed in on her batting the kind of beautiful long, glossy eyelashes we've all stood in front of the mirror and wished for at some point in our lives. But before you rush out and buy yourself this magical cosmetic hoping to be transformed into a Cruz look-alike, literally with the wave of mini wand, you might be interested to know that in Britain the Advertising Standards Authority found that the ads were misleading because nowhere did they state that Cruz was wearing . . . false eyelashes. In response to the complaints, L'Oreal said that using fake eyelashes in ads was "common industry practice." Oh, well, that makes me feel so much better.

What Julia Roberts Knows About Information Technologies

Celebrities are used to sell just about everything. But you have to stop and ask yourself: What expertise do they have? Julia Roberts has done a series of voiceovers for AOL ads—but when did she have time to become an IT expert? (In between *Ocean's 11* and *Ocean's 12*, perhaps?) "Because Julia Roberts told me to" doesn't sound like a logical reason for me to choose AOL over another Internet service provider. At least when Martha Stewart makes a line of bed sheets, I feel like I'm buying from someone who not only knows the product she is selling but has painstakingly investigated every thread in the factory. I can picture her yelling, "Loom faster!" or "Higher thread count, nobody gets out of here until we reach Egyptian standards!" Even if it isn't true, it feels true . . . after all, what foolish production supervisor would risk getting on the wrong side of Martha Stewart?

Are glamorous stars such as Sarah Jessica Parker and Eva Longoria really in a position to advise you on which brand of home hair dye works best?

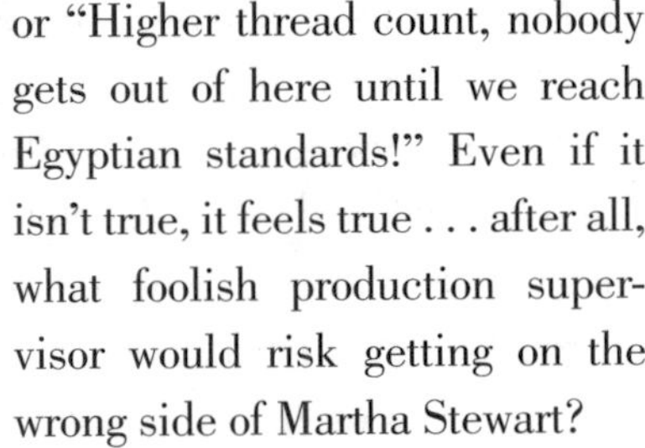

Are glamorous stars such as Sarah Jessica Parker and Eva Longoria really in a position to advise you on which brand of home hair dye works best—I mean, *honestly*, can you picture them donning those useless plastic gloves they always give you, leaning over the bathroom sink, struggling not to end up with a brunette forehead and ears?

Gene Hackman is the spokesperson for Lowes Home Improvement, but what is his expertise in this field? I think you'd be a little shocked if he showed up at your door to hang dry wall. Even Harrison Ford would have been a more realistic choice—at least he at some point in his life was in construction.

Jay-Z, Serena Williams, and Gwen Stefani have all done ads for Hewlett-Packard. . . . *Why*? I don't think any one of them knows the difference between a microchip and a potato chip (hint Gwen, one of them is made out of potato).

Gwyneth Paltrow is known for her great acting ability and her even greater taste in men, but she has never been known for her great beauty, yet Estée Lauder reportedly paid the Oscar winner over $30 million to be the face of their company. This is despite the fact that she told *USA Today*, "I don't tend to wear a lot of makeup in my daily life," and has also been caught saying she isn't a big makeup fan.

Sometimes, though, advertisers have to face facts: There are certain purchasing decisions where we won't take a celebrity's word for it. This is nowhere more evident than in the marketing of cars, big-ticket items where we need more than just the positive association of a big star.

General Motors (GM) paid Tiger Woods a whopping $40 million to convince us that he would drive a Buick—a Buick?!—and that we all should too. It's a great car, but I just can't picture Woods driving a Buick. This is the guy who was number two on the *Forbes* list of most powerful athletes a few years back, when he was making $87 million a year. Am I to believe that one day while out car shopping, Woods bypassed the Maserati dealership to get himself a Buick? Unlikely. Especially given that at the same time he had a Rolex watch endorsement deal. If you are creating an image, shouldn't it be consistent? A Buick and a Rolex? I don't think so, and neither did the public. To save face, a GM spokesperson told *USA Today* that they would use Tiger in their corporate-level marketing instead and that they "don't want a celebrity at the core of any brand. We want the message on Buick to be about Buick."

In GM's case, it was that the product didn't match the celebrity, but what about when the celebrity eclipses the product? This was the case when Chrysler paid Celine Dion $14 million to do a series of lovely black-and-white television commercials for several of their car models. The ads did wonders for sales of Dion's new CD, but it seems no one noticed the cars.

Check the label. A celebrity's endorsement doesn't make a brand any better or worse than another brand. It may, however, make it more expensive. The acne medication Proactiv has the same active ingredient (benzoyl peroxide) as other preparations you can buy at the pharmacy for a fraction of the price. Both of them successfully clear up mild acne. The major difference, however, seems to be that the cheaper products don't have Jessica Simpson, Jennifer Love Hewitt, Vanessa Williams, and Serena Williams rhapsodizing about them in advertisements. The company told a *Today Show* reporter in 2006 that Proactiv has a unique formulation and manufacturing procedures, but when a dermatologist compared the results of a woman who used the celebrity-endorsed product for a month and another who used cheap pharmacy products, he judged them to be on par.

CHAPTER SEVEN

Rock My World Then Save It

Look, I would much rather people were listening to politicians about this than actors, but the politicians aren't talking about this.

MATT DAMON, SPEAKING ABOUT CHILD POVERTY AND DISEASE IN AFRICA IN *MACLEAN'S* MAGAZINE, NOVEMBER 2007

How much easier life must have been for celebrities during the golden age of Hollywood, when a star just had to be a star. No one expected Gloria Swanson to roll up the sleeves of her mink coat and hand out aid to orphans in Africa. Cary Grant could drink martinis all night long if he felt like it. He never had to show up for a UN meeting the next morning or hop a red-eye to go lobby Congress. When Marilyn Monroe crashed and burned, she left behind a legend, not a handful of charitable trusts and foundations. And all that was fine with us.

Stars played heroes in Hollywood movies, but we expected real people to take on the job of heroes—great wartime leaders such as Franklin Delano Roosevelt and Winston Churchill, civil rights campaigners such as Martin Luther King Jr. and Rosa Parks. We looked to religious leaders and elders in our own communities for inspiration and social guidance. It wasn't the job of a celebrity to save the world or show us how to be the best we can be. The job of a celebrity was to entertain us and be glamorous.

Now a growing group of A-list stars seem to spend just as much time performing as they do campaigning for social justice, finding cures for diseases, ending world debt, and saving the environment. In turn the C- and D-listers feel that if they don't align themselves with a charity or commit to a world-saving cause, well . . . they're never going to be famous. And it's not only the bleeding-heart liberal lefties, it's all celebrities, no matter which way they lean or whom they support politically. They are no one without a charitable affiliation. Being a good performer or great beauty is no longer enough; a star has to be a humanitarian.

Advocacy has also become the way to get back into the good graces of the American people, especially if you've screwed up publicly. Even Paris Hilton made a humanitarian effort, or at least aimed a promise in that direction, after her twenty-three-day jail stay in 2007. She was going to save orphans, or somebody in Rwanda, she wasn't sure. (Maybe she had been advised that they were wearing last year's look, or she found out they didn't have Starbucks there.) The trip never happened, but when even the Paris Hiltons of the world recognize the value of being—or at least being seen as—a humanitarian, you know something big is happening.

The Celebrity-hero

Based on what you see in the media, often it seems that celebrities are the ones who work the hardest to make the world a better place. Darfur, global warming, third-world debt, finding a cure for life-threatening diseases—when you think of these things, do you think of politicians, diplomats, and religious or community leaders? Or do you think of George Clooney, Angelina Jolie, Bono, Michael J. Fox, and Lance Armstrong?

At a time when politicians and community leaders seem to have given up on solving the big problems, have humanitarian celebrities stepped into the vacuum? Have they become our new heroes?

Mike Farrell, best known for playing Captain B. J. Hunnicutt in the Emmy Award–winning series *M*A*S*H*, has long been involved with human rights, immigration issues, children's rights, and an impressive list of social programs. I asked him whether celebrities can replace politicians as the people we look to for solutions to the world's problems, as the people we look to as heroes.

"The good politicians, those who truly understand and believe in the value of public service, all too often find their motives questioned by a public made cynical by the lies, corruption, and self-serving behavior of too many of their colleagues. Those among them who maintain their integrity in the face of this cynicism can still triumph," says Farrell. "This overarching distrust hasn't yet completely enveloped the celebrity world, so those who continue

"Overarching distrust hasn't yet completely enveloped the celebrity world, so [celebrities can] provide examples of caring, of positive behavior, and even . . . of heroism."

—MIKE FARRELL

to enjoy a degree of public trust can, if willing, provide examples of caring, of positive behavior, and even . . . of heroism."

In 2005 a group of psychologists researched attitudes toward celebrities and heroes, and their work was published in the *British Journal of Psychology*. They had asked 299 Brits between the ages of eighteen and seventy-seven to nominate their favorite hero and their favorite celebrity. They found that people categorized the two separately, coming up with two distinctly different sets of names. The top five heroes were Winston Churchill, Nelson Mandela, Martin Luther King Jr., Diana Princess of Wales, and Jesus, while the top five celebrities were soccer star David Beckham, comedian and actor Billy Connolly, Michael Jackson, Sean Connery, and pop singer Robbie Williams—okay, okay, the Brits have peculiar taste in celebrities, but you get the idea.

What interests me is the way the researchers defined *hero* and *celebrity*. When participants nominated a hero, it had to be someone who did something of lasting value for the world. Their favorite celebrity, on the other hand, was to be someone who merely entertained and produced work that was relatively fleeting in its impact. In defining heroes and celebrities that way, were the researchers working with an outdated concept of celebrity?

Perhaps in the future researchers will have to take a whole new category into consideration when they ask this kind of question—the celebrity-hero who blurs the line between merely entertaining his or her fans and leaving a legacy that will make him or her a hero to future generations.

The idea of a celebrity as someone who simply entertains us in a trivial way is evolving into something more substantial. Some stars remain famous only for their talents (or for their misbehavior), and they will probably pass from people's memories as the years go on. But there is a growing number of stars who are setting up schools, helping eradicate AIDS or global warming, and fighting to cure cancer or spinal cord injuries. They will leave behind not just popular movies or albums but charitable trusts and foundations that will live on in perpetuity. While future generations may forget what they were famous for, their names will be forever in the public eye, in big letters on the front of hospitals, schools, and animal shelters, or in scholarships, grants, and charities. These may be the first stars who never fade.

Stay informed. Learn about the issues affecting you, your community, and your environment and then decide for yourself which issues *you* consider to be the most important—don't just take your favorite celebrity's word for it. When you have a cause you care about, go to GoodSearch.com powered by Yahoo! The site donates 50 percent of its revenue to charities designated by its users.

Perhaps one of the earliest examples of a celebrity doing good for the world during a non-wartime era was Danny Kaye, who in 1956 became UNICEF's first-ever Goodwill Ambassador. (A number of celebrities have been Goodwill Ambassadors since then, but the most famous must be Audrey Hepburn, who succeeded Kaye in 1988.) Many stars in the past were known to contribute to charities, but back then the fund-raising events were informal: Gene Kelly, Bob Hope, Ronald Reagan, and Frank Sinatra getting together on the spur of the moment for a charity baseball game, or the time, according to a November 2000 *New York Times* article,

Sinatra read about a destitute family with seven kids during the holidays and impulsively sent them a plane loaded with food, clothes, presents, and a Christmas tree.

But things began to change in the 1980s. Celebrities became more directly and prominently involved in social and world events, and their involvement became more than just writing a check to an organization; it became championing a cause and becoming the face of that cause. The world had never seen anything quite like Bob Geldof's 1985 Live Aid to help the hungry in Ethiopia. Geldof galvanized a slew of celebrities into action and paved the way for future megastar campaigners such as Bono, Sting, and Peter Gabriel.

This was the time when celebrities became the barometer for the zeitgeist of society. If you wanted to know what was happening, what social movement was about to unfold, you knew who to look to—and it wasn't the politicos. Case in point: Another big news story that had been brewing in the 1980s was the new deadly disease HIV-AIDS. When Rock Hudson died of AIDS, Elizabeth Taylor spearheaded a movement to raise awareness and funds, and she has since been followed by everyone from Elton John to Sharon Stone. At first the disease appeared to be something that affected mainly homosexual men, but scientists soon discovered that anyone was vulnerable if not careful; however, the general public was slow to catch up. It wasn't until about a decade after the discovery of HIV that another celebrity would have a valuable impact on the public's awareness and understanding of the disease.

The Magic Johnson Effect

In November 1991, legendary basketball star and heterosexual male Ervin "Magic" Johnson announced that he was HIV positive, presenting a new image to the American public of what HIV looks like. In a press conference at the Great Western Forum, where he played with the Lakers for twelve seasons, Johnson said, "Because of the HIV virus I have obtained, I will have to announce my retirement from the Lakers today. . . . I am saying it can happen to anybody, even me, Magic Johnson." *Newsweek* interviewed fans who said they had been "crying for two days," others who were simply confounded. His supporters reacted passionately. The *Newsweek* article reported that the National AIDS Hotline received 40,000 calls the day after Johnson's speech instead of their usual 3,800, and the Centers for Disease Control, which normally gets about 200 calls per hour, received 10,000 in a single hour on the night of the announcement. *Newsweek* called it "the biggest thing to happen to AIDS since Rock Hudson."

Not only did Johnson's statement have an impact on his fans, it put psychology and sociology researchers into a frenzy as well. In the years following this news, study after study pondered a phenomenon now referred to as "the Magic Johnson Effect."

Other stars have had public battles with serious illnesses, but Johnson's was in a class all its own, because as a heterosexual African-American living out every part of the American Dream, Johnson defied the stereotype of who gets HIV. His announcement had a profound impact on high-risk youth who previously were immune to messages about the disease.

Peter Scales, Ph.D., of the Search Institute, which is devoted to educating people about childhood and adolescent development, believes that Johnson's announcement had a powerful effect because "he is an exception that proves the rule. Magic is a well-respected and well-loved individual, loved for his personality and warmth long before HIV, with basketball skills that transcended the sport. When he faced adversity he had millions of people who cared and watched how he would handle it, and we saw his sense of mission for other people. Not many athletes today have that kind of respect for character."

A study published in 1996 in the journal *Adolescence* (and other later studies) looked at whether Johnson changed the attitudes of young people who had little knowledge of HIV-AIDS, didn't normally attend treatment clinics, or distrusted the medical community. They found that a year after Johnson's disclosure, 60 percent of these young people who visited clinics had an increased awareness of AIDS and HIV. More than 65 percent said they took it upon themselves in a sexual situation to make sure they were protected, and almost 40 percent of girls said that they now resisted sexual peer pressure.

This was the impact that Johnson's announcement and his subsequent involvement in HIV-AIDS awareness campaigns had on his fans. These were kids who had no experience with HIV and AIDS and thought that it was a disease for homosexuals, which for the most part they were not. Up until then these kids had also resisted the notion that it was a disease that reached all races and ethnicities.

Johnson boosted public awareness that the heterosexual population could contract HIV, and because he was so well liked, he wielded social influence. And just as Courtney Love's honesty after the suicide of her husband, Kurt Cobain, positively influenced Cobain's fans, Johnson's full disclosure and honest approach to a frightening situation made all the difference. His ability to be upfront about something very personal bonded him to his fans in a new way. Keep in mind: This was at a time when stars were still fairly secretive about their private lives. We didn't have the glut of celebrity weeklies, tabloids, Web sites, and information about celebrities circulating like we do now. Johnson's HIV awareness raising had an amazing impact, made all the more powerful because the public had never been let into a star's life quite like this before.

Cause Celeb

If Johnson was a pioneer, then numerous other celebrities suffering from serious diseases have taken a cue from him, setting up their own foundations to raise awareness and fund research into a whole range of life-threatening diseases. Former cycling champion Lance Armstrong has not only raised awareness of testicular cancer, he has also become a tireless campaigner, fighting on behalf of all people with cancer. In 2004 his yellow Livestrong wristbands started the huge fund-raising and social phenomenon that has seen brightly colored charity wristbands appearing on the arms of everyone from the person standing in front of you in line at the grocery store to presidential hopefuls.

Christopher Reeve, who became a quadriplegic after a horseback riding accident in 1995, devoted the final decade of his life to raising funds and fighting for changes to the laws relating to stem cell research, to aid people with spinal cord injuries. He appeared before Congress as a patient advocate. Michael J. Fox continues to lobby for stem cell research, but his goal is a cure for Parkinson's disease, which he was diagnosed with in 1991. He has appeared before Congress and a Senate subcommittee and lobbied senators to pass the Stem Cell Research Enhancement Act, which they did, in April 2007.

The stories of these three stars can be seen in a heroic light. Certainly they were in line to benefit from advances in these fields of medicine, but they didn't *have* to work hard—perhaps harder than they ever did in the careers that made them famous—in order to help everyone who has or is at risk of these illnesses. In the case of Reeve, it must have been physically difficult for him to campaign. Perhaps he became in real life far more of a hero than his character Superman ever was. According to his Web site, www.christopherreeve.org, Reeve once said that when

"I think of a hero as an ordinary individual who finds the strength to persevere and endure in spite of overwhelming obstacles."

—CHRISTOPHER REEVE

the first *Superman* movie was released, interviewers kept asking him "What is a hero?" At the time he said that "a hero is someone who commits a courageous action without considering the consequences," but after his accident he said, "Now my definition is completely different. I think of a hero as an ordinary individual who finds the strength to persevere and endure in spite of overwhelming obstacles. They are the real heroes, and so are the families and friends who have stood by them."

Given the severity of his symptoms, it also seems pretty heroic that Michael J. Fox continues to rally for support. In *Case Studies in Health Communication*, Christina Beck, an expert in health communication at Ohio University, writes, "Of course, I don't really know Michael J. Fox, but I rejoiced at the news of his wedding and grieved over news of his health challenge. I'm not an obsessed 'nut'; I'm just a fan, similar to millions of other fans, who come to care about someone who seems deceptively near through the magical intimacy of contemporary media and popular culture. . . . Connectedness with fans fosters fame and, in the event of illness or injury, opportunity to translate stardom into public awareness and political advocacy."

Perhaps another aspect of these men's heroism is that they had the courage to show their vulnerability to the world, when fans were used to seeing them at the top of their game with their star personas switched on. According to communication researcher Mary Casey and her colleagues, that's the difference between a celebrity endorsing a product and a celebrity endorsing a health message. While celebrity ads for cola or mascara rely on the *persona* of the star, communicating a health message is all about shedding the persona and revealing the *personal* side of the star.

It seems that celebrity branding plays just as important a role in promoting public health as it does in advertising and marketing products. In a 2003 study that appeared in the *Journal of Health Communication,* William Brown, professor and research fellow at Regent University, says "When a celebrity becomes closely aligned with a health issue, like Christopher Reeve and stem cell research, or Michael J. Fox and Parkinson's disease, then the media attention given to that celebrity draws public involvement into his or her health issue. . . . Just as products are branded with the help of celebrity endorsements . . . perhaps celebrities may brand even specific diseases."

Ladies, I don't mean to single out the men as heroes. There are plenty of female celebrity health warriors who are just as much heroes as Armstrong, Reeve, and Fox. In 2005, one year after Christopher Reeve's death, his wife, Dana, was named Mother of the Year by the American Cancer Society. At the time, she was raising her son singlehanded, running the Christopher Reeve Foundation, and raising awareness of lung cancer, which took her life in 2006 despite the fact she had never smoked. Not to mention the candor, courage, and hard work of the many female celebrities—such as Sheryl Crow, Edie Falco, Melissa Etheridge, Suzanne Somers, and Olivia Newton-John—who have survived breast cancer and gone public about it.

Practice early detection and prevention. If increased awareness of celebrity illnesses means that the public is more likely to seek testing and treatment, or change their lifestyle, that's a positive thing. And if you have an illness, you should take comfort and strength from whatever sources you can find—and sometimes that includes inspirational celebrities who are also fighting or have survived a similar health crisis.

But don't forget to pay attention to less high-profile health issues. Heart disease is the leading killer in this country, and stroke and diabetes also take a heavy toll, yet they tend not to capture the headlines. They might not have as many celebrities championing them, but they do take thousands of lives each year. And in many cases, you can reduce your risk with straightforward lifestyle changes, preventative testing, and awareness.

Does all this extra public awareness make us look after our health better? Just as Johnson encouraged people to find out more about preventing HIV, it seems that celebrities do influence people to go for cancer screening tests. A study in the *Journal of the National Cancer Institute* in 2005 showed that hearing Katie Couric talk about getting a colonoscopy made people 37 percent more likely to go have that test. Similar responses were seen when women heard Nancy Reagan and Rosie O'Donnell talk about the need for mammograms, and when men heard Norman Schwarzkopf talk about prostate cancer screening. A 2005 study reported in the *Medical Journal of Australia* found that there was a 40 percent increase in bookings for mammograms for two weeks following the news that the country's biggest pop star, Kylie Minogue, was diagnosed with breast cancer. And if even one of those people had cancer detected early and got life-saving treatment, that's a good thing.

For some, working for a cause may help them mollify their guilt over having great success, for others it seems it's true benevolence.

When Oprah opened up on her show about her battles with menopause and her thyroid condition, the story made its way to the celebrity entertainment news. Viewers responded to Oprah's revelations in the same way they do whenever a female celebrity comes out and says, "I have breast cancer": They went to their doctors. Many of these women were, like Oprah, leading busy lives—perhaps juggling a career, children, or aging parents, meanwhile neglecting their own health. A wake-up call from a respected celebrity such as Oprah can be crucial to getting people to the doctor's office for treatment.

Not Just Skin Deep

The field of skin care tends to be strongly influenced by celebrities, but not only in the way you might expect. Fifth Avenue dermatologist Diane Madfes says that patients do sometimes come in holding photos of their favorite stars, asking for treatments to make their eyes or lips match the photos. Madfes sees potential medical benefits to these celebrity-inspired trends, benefits that go far deeper than the cosmetic level: It causes patients to think more about protecting their skin and encourages them to visit their doctor. While lasering and injecting, a doctor can check patients for skin cancer, which is the third most common cancer and treatable if detected early. Madfes's message is this: "Many people feel they already did the damage, but it's not too late!" While you are there for Botox—which according to Madfes was a celebrity trend that crossed over into the general public—have a full body check.

The Mighty Casey Helps Out

While it may be easy to understand why celebrities who have illnesses work so hard to champion their cause and make a difference, it's not always clear why some healthy and fit celebrities choose to do the same. For some, working for a cause may help them mollify their guilt over having great success, for others it seems to be true benevolence. The real question is: Does their social campaigning actually affect the way we think and act?

Regent University Professor William J. Brown and his team tried to answer this question by studying the attitudes of almost 400 Mark McGwire fans between the ages of eighteen and forty. For those of you nonsporting types (like myself), McGwire was a major league baseball player, who in 1998 held the home run record, received an enormous amount of publicity, and was, according to Brown, "instantly declared an American hero and held up as a positive role model for teenagers and young adults."

He also happened to campaign for child abuse prevention, and the study aimed to find out whether he influenced people's awareness of this issue. Indeed the researchers found that a significant number of people said that McGwire had made them more aware of the issue and helped them realize that it's important to speak out against child abuse. They also found that people who were already fans of McGwire were the most strongly influenced—so, the more popular the star, the more influential he or she can be in changing attitudes and behavior.

Brown and his colleagues found that people tend to imitate celebrities "as a way of maintaining a desired relationship" with them. By saying what our favorite stars say, doing what they do, believing what they believe, we can maintain a relationship with them, which in turn helps us define ourselves. By identifying with stars, by adopting their attitudes and altruistic ideals, fans can connect with their heroes.

But celebrity influence is a double-edged sword. If you can be positively influenced by a celebrity's message, you can be negatively influenced, too. In addition to being known for his child advocacy program, the Mark McGwire Foundation for Children, McGwire was also publicly known to use performance-enhancing anabolic steroids. At the time McGwire became the home run record holder, such drugs were not banned in baseball—in other sports, yes, but not yet in baseball.

While 13 percent of people surveyed reported that McGwire influenced them to speak out against child abuse, *65 percent* of them reported that they were aware of his steroid use. If celebrities can influence us to care about social issues, they can also influence us toward drug use. "As a credit to McGwire," said the researchers, "he stopped using Androstenedione as soon as he heard that young people were emulating his behavior."

The Global Celeb Community

The developing world is a major area where celebrities have raised public awareness. The Rwandan genocide is considered one of the most complex and horrific humanitarian crises of the 1990s, yet some people had never even heard of the Tutsi or Hutu tribes until they saw Don Cheadle's performance in 2004's *Hotel Rwanda.* Did it have to receive Oscar nominations for some of us to find out what had happened in that part of the world? Thank goodness Hollywood cares: Entire generations have been educated about the world not through reading newspapers or class discussions at school but through film. Blood diamonds? That was a fringe issue until Leonardo DiCaprio starred in a movie about it and began speaking out publicly. Now many women are looking at their engagement rings thinking, hmm, did someone lose a hand so I could have this?

Even when there is no link to their career, some stars draw attention to issues. The Darfur crisis was unfolding for years but barely rated a mention until celebrities such as Clooney and Cheadle became interested. For most of us, third-world debt might have seemed simply inevitable until Bono put the question out there: Could the world's wealthier nations in fact forgive some of that debt or do more to help poorer countries get back on their feet? And then there's Angelina Jolie, who seems to spend more time traveling the globe looking for people to help than she does looking for movie roles.

The world community didn't listen about Darfur; some world leaders continued to disbelieve there even was such a thing as global warming.

Oprah is perhaps the gold standard in celebrity philanthropy, giving to local and overseas causes. Each year the Giving Back Fund, a charity devoted to encouraging philanthropy in the entertainment and sports industries, compiles a list of the biggest celebrity donors. In 2007 they ranked Oprah number one; she had given $58.3 million to her Oprah's Angel Network and Leadership Academy in South Africa, a 50-acre $40 million venture that provides its 450 students with textbooks, meals, and an opportunity to dream, become something, and most important, get out of desperate poverty.

Environmentalism is another huge issue taken up by celebrities, perhaps most notably by DiCaprio, who set up his own foundation in 1998, the Leonardo DiCaprio Foundation, and has made several documentaries on saving the planet. His Web site (www.leonardodicaprio.com) is not the usual Hollywood PR puff page . . . his home page has two sides, one about his career, the other entirely devoted to environmental causes. This is clearly much more than a hobby for him.

These celebrities are like pioneering heroes, stepping in to fill a gap because politicians and the global community have failed to solve these problems. The world community didn't listen about Darfur, and some world leaders continued to disbelieve there even was such a thing as global warming. How much the public's and our leaders' attitudes have changed thanks to celebrity activism is impossible to quantify, but there have certainly been big shifts in our attitudes toward the plight of the developing world.

Issue Fatigue

There are now so many celebrity UN Goodwill Ambassadors that the position seems to have become a revolving door, if not a résumé requirement. Which begs the question: Is the title *UN Goodwill Ambassador* losing its meaning?

Another celebrity trend, for want of a better word, is going to Africa and returning with a baby. Overseas adoption is a serious business, and no doubt the stars considered those adoptions long and hard beforehand, the way we would too. But because of all the media we are exposed to, celebrity stories tend to blur together, hiding the fact that each star's adoption decision is a carefully considered, individual success story. It has become acceptable for the media to speak of celebrity adoptions disparagingly—at least for the late-night comics, whose job it is to make jokes at the expense of celebrities (even those who are trying to save young lives). At the 2006 Academy Awards, Jon Stewart quipped, "This broadcast is being viewed by millions of people, nearly half of which are in the process of being adopted by Angelina Jolie."

Get inspired. When you see a celebrity doing something that you think is worthy and good, turn it into action in your own community. Sometimes it may look as though philanthropy is only possible if you have a spare few hundred million and can build a school or hospital in an impoverished country. But you don't have to have bundles of cash to help others. There are plenty of volunteer groups working for the good of your community right now who are asking for nothing but a little of your time. And you don't have to be Al Gore or Leonardo DiCaprio to help save the environment. Each little step you take at home (changing to environmentally friendly light bulbs, recycling, taking your own bags when you do the grocery shopping) adds up. My good friend David Frei of the Westminster Kennel Club suggests, "If you love dogs, go to your local ASPCA or animal shelter and train the dogs waiting for homes so that when potential adopting families come by, they see a good dog and will more likely want to take him home."

With so many celebrities attached to so many causes, are we at the point where causes don't mean as much to us as they used to and passionate celebrity advocates are nothing but late-night fodder? There is an entire body of research into how violence on TV and in video games desensitizes us to real violence—but what about constant exposure to celebrity causes desensitizing us to the issues? We know through years of study that advertising tends to lose its effectiveness when we are swamped by hundreds of different ads each day. Let's hope the same thing does not happen here and that as the number of celebrities with causes grows, our attention span for each does not shrink.

International Adoption

Although the media often portray a celebrity international adoption as a simple, spontaneous act, in fact it is a complex process that can involve many legal and bureaucratic steps. The State Department cautions that an international adoption is considered a private matter between the adopting parents and the foreign court, operating under the specific laws and policies of that country. Authorities in the United States cannot intervene on behalf of prospective parents in their dealings with foreign courts, but the State Department does provide extensive information about the process of international adoption.

A tiny proportion of Americans adopt children. With all of the children in this world who need homes and families, we should all think twice before judging Mia Farrow, Madonna, or Brad and Angelina because they put their strollers where their mouths are.

CHAPTER EIGHT

Celebritocracy

Vote or Die!

Sean "P. Diddy" Combs

We have all become accustomed to celebrities voicing their political opinions at awards ceremonies, on their impassioned blogs, or while hosting charity events. In that egalitarian and supportive atmosphere, there is a certain impropriety in a celebrity launching into a speech about Tibet or Iraq or the death penalty while clutching a shiny statuette and adjusting the straps of her designer evening gown. While some of us might not appreciate politics mixed in with our entertainment, we haven't been *that* bothered, because after all, awards season doesn't last forever. We could always take refuge in politician-only celebrity-free media zones. But even that is changing.

C-SPAN gives the public access to the political process, allowing us to be flies on the wall of our democracy in action, but lately it leaves me wondering if there is a red carpet on Capitol Hill that I was unaware of. These days C-SPAN is looking more like *Access Hollywood* than a place to watch a six-hour debate on farm subsidies. (You can almost hear the voiceover, "Today on a very special C-SPAN . . . ") Granted, celebrity advocacy makes perfect sense under some circumstances, such as when Muhammad Ali appeared before Congress to appeal for additional funding for Parkinson's research, a disease he is afflicted with. But on another . . . ummm . . . episode . . . a random Backstreet Boy was there calling for relief from coal slurry. Huh?

According to CBS News, the "boy" in question was Kevin Richardson, who had concerns on behalf of his environmental group Just Within Reach. He and his perfect hair came to testify on the subject of mountaintop removal mining, which according to Grist.org is a coal-extraction process devastating Appalachia. Even though this Backstreet Boy hails from Kentucky coal-mining country, I suspect his presence on Capitol Hill had a lot to do with his star status. In the powerful world of Washington, D.C., lobbyists, what really counts is that he brought attention and media coverage to the issue. That's why celebrity and politics have such a close alliance: No one else can capture the public's attention quite like a celebrity. And as celebrity's hold grows stronger on us every day, the alliance between celebrity and politics inevitably draws closer.

All over the world wars are being fought for the right to live in a democracy, but in this country those battles were fought and won long ago. We each have a right to our own opinion, a right to have our voice heard, a right to influence how the country is run. This right is for *all* of us, not just for the politicians or the celebrities who increasingly dominate the public stage. Your own civic responsibility is to find out the facts, formulate your own opinion, and feel free to shout it from the rooftops.

But in a celebrity-saturated world, how loud is your voice? Is it as loud as famously outspoken celebrities such as Susan Sarandon, Barbra Streisand, or Robert Duvall? Do you have as much chance of influencing the policies of your political party as Charlton Heston, who not only donated thousands of dollars cash each year but also appeared at election campaign events, lending his formidable fame to the occasion?

In a sense, perhaps we elect our favorite celebrities—we vote for them on *American Idol*, we choose whether to buy their records or tickets to see their movies—but is that enough? Do celebrities wield too much political power? Are we living in a celebritocracy?

In a celebrity-saturated world, how loud is your voice?

Lobby for what you believe in. Your leaders were elected to represent you, so tell them how you feel and what you want from them. Write letters, start petitions, join lobby groups, send e-mails and faxes; however you want to contact them—let them hear from you! Your timing is important, however. Watch for special periods in the legislative process when your letters and e-mails can be especially productive, such as when a bill is introduced and assigned to a committee. Let your legislators know you want them to cosponsor the bill.

There are other ways to make your voice heard. Of course I am a huge advocate of radio call-in shows. I also love the idea of a well-put letter to the editor.

How It All Began

Actor and activist Mike Farrell believes that celebrities can have a positive influence on the world. He tells me, "I would love to see more attention paid (and here the media could actually do some good) to the true heroes in our society. Those who too often struggle unnoticed in the trenches of social injustice attempting to teach our children, feed, clothe, and harbor the hungry and homeless, bind our wounds and inspire an understanding and appreciation of fundamental human value." To that end celebrity and politics can be quite a beneficial coupling, the origins of which are as fascinating as any social movement in American history.

God Bless America

Celebrity's influence on politics is hardly new—it's just slicker, more organized, and harder to escape than ever before. Probably the first person in this country to highlight the merging of celebrity and politics was Columbia University professor Robert K. Merton, one of the giants of sociology, back in the 1940s.

Merton illustrated how powerfully the public's opinion can be swayed by a celebrity in his 1946 book *Mass Persuasion.* He described the profound impact Kate Smith, a very popular singer of the 1930s and 1940s, had on the American public during wartime. Millions heard Smith's weekly radio show, the *Kate Smith Hour,* and the public simply went crazy for her rendition of Irving Berlin's "God Bless America." Such was this star's influence that when she began to sing the tune during every broadcast as a way of raising money for war bonds, the public obeyed her requests and donated over $600 million—an incredible amount of money even by current standards—which went to help the U.S.'s military efforts in World War II.

Smith's passionate singing even spawned a movement to make "God Bless America" our national anthem. The movement picked up so much steam that the lyrics were introduced into the Congressional Record, but Smith addressed Congress and implored them not to change the national anthem, arguing that since the "Star Spangled Banner" had been written during wartime, it should remain.

Smith was so crucial to the government's World War II propaganda machine that when President Roosevelt introduced her to the King of England, America's wartime ally, he said simply: "This is Kate Smith. Miss Smith is America." Even forty years after the war, politicians still recognized the role she played. According to the *New York Times Magazine,* upon her death in 1986, President Reagan saw fit to mark her passing, saying, "Kate Smith was a patriot in every sense of the word." (Proceeds from her version of "God Bless America" now go to the Girl Scouts and Boy Scouts of America.)

Yes, Celebrity Endorsement Really Is a Political Strategy

Smith may no longer be the celebrity on everybody's lips, but in recent decades there has certainly been no shortage of stars trying to influence public opinion. Bill Clinton's 1993 inauguration parties looked less like political soirees and more like a celebrity outreach program. The luminaries who joined in the inauguration celebrations that week included, in no particular order: Diana Ross, Jack Nicholson reciting Abraham Lincoln, Aretha Franklin performing a song from *Les Miserables,* Kermit the Frog, Barbra Streisand (of course), Warren Beatty, En Vogue and Boys II Men doing a cappella versions of "The Star-Spangled Banner," Michael Jackson, Fleetwood Mac, Oprah, Little Richard, Kenny Rogers, Bill Cosby, opera singer Kathleen Battle, Macaulay Culkin, Harry Belafonte, Chuck

Berry, L. L. Cool J, Goldie Hawn, Quincy Jones, and Bob Dylan. It was easy to forget these were political events, not concerts.

What I always wanted to know was whether such celebrity endorsements are just a happy coincidence for politicians, or if the politicos actually go out and court the stars. Sure, politicians know that having celebs on their side adds a certain cache to their campaign—but is it a deliberate strategy?

The answer lies with a man named Alan R. Novak, who back in the 1960s was senior counsel to Democratic Senator Edward M. Kennedy. In 1964, after John F. Kennedy had been assassinated and Lyndon Johnson had become president, Novak sent a very telling memo to Clifton Carter, President Johnson's chief fund-raiser and executive director of the Democratic National Committee.

"The entertainment world is solidly in the Democratic camp," he wrote. "These people, traditionally liberal, were in the past issue-oriented. . . . This year, as a result of Goldwater's candidacy, performers as a group are now identifying themselves with a party—the Democrats." He went on to explain that a conversation he'd had with actor Paul Newman opened his eyes to an amazing campaign strategy. Apparently Newman had told Novak that "a substantial number of performers are ready, willing and able to donate their services for campaign activities. Mr. Newman has indicated a willingness to take on a large burden of the recruitment on the East Coast and has indicated that Steve Allen, or someone like him, could be enlisted for the same task on the West Coast." He concluded, "There is no shortage of recruiters within the entertainment world."

Novak argued in the memo that a celebrity's participation in a politician's campaign can be measured "in dollars and cents" and "substantial campaign contributions." Celebrities also bring other, less tangible benefits, because they can "add glamour to the

Democratic campaign and to the Democratic nominees, increase the prospects of broad media coverage . . . and add vigor to the programs on which performers are appearing, placing the audience in a receptive mood for the political speeches, with which the entertainment could be integrated." But like advertisers who have to be wary that a celebrity's indiscretions will reflect poorly on their products, political candidates need to be cautious, too. Novak added a chilling caveat to his memo: "Not all performers would contribute to the image the Party is striving to create. Screening, of course, would be necessary." Brilliant.

Political parties and pundits take the relationship between candidates and celebrities so seriously that in 2007, *Forbes* magazine felt it was necessary to add a whole new category to their opinion polling on presidential hopefuls: Which celebs would be good for a campaign and which ones political poison? Based on the results, they warned candidates to steer clear of Rosie O'Donnell, Tom Cruise, Madonna, Jane Fonda, Donald Trump, and Susan Sarandon but run, don't walk, to get Oprah, Tom Hanks, George Clooney, Jon Stewart, Angelina Jolie, and Tiger Woods on their side.

They warned candidates to steer clear of Rosie O'Donnell, Tom Cruise, Madonna, Jane Fonda, Donald Trump, and Susan Sarandon.

Who's Left, Who's Right?

Actors are notoriously Democrat. If you look at campaign contributions over the last ten years or so, you find that a great deal of actors and Hollywood producers support the Democrats. According to the Federal Election Commission, since 1993 producer Steve Bing, the father of Elizabeth Hurley's baby, has given over $10 million to the Democratic Party and their candidates almost exclusively. Sports stars and country music stars, along with a few comedians, tend to support Republican candidates. It's probably no surprise that *Access Hollywood's* Billy Bush, who happens to be a cousin of George W., gives to the GOP. Perhaps more surprisingly, Candace Bushnell, of *Sex and the City* and *Lipstick Jungle* fame, has also donated to the Republicans—and Bob Barker has, too.

Money is like oxygen to a political campaign. Without ample financing, candidates cannot fund advertising, pay their campaign staff, or trek back and forth across the country to kiss babies, shake hands, and sample regional fast-food delicacies. The size of their bank balance also affects how we see candidates. And the bigger and more glamorous the celebrity fund-raiser is, the more media coverage the campaign will get.

When it comes to running for office, we see that Hollywood does have a Conservative side after all. Conservative actors are the ones who actually get up and do it—Ronald Reagan, Arnold Schwarzenegger, Fred "Gopher" Grandy, Clint Eastwood, Sonny Bono, Fred Thompson. While liberal Hollywood seems to be mostly interested in lobbying for political beliefs and helping finance Democrat campaigns, the Hollywood Republican minority seems to be more driven to actually seize power. Is there something about being a leading man or playing a hero on screen that makes it easier for voters to picture a candidate leading their state or country? Studies say, "Absolutely."

According to the journal *Gender & Society*, it was Schwarzenegger's symbolic masculine persona that got him elected in 2003. He crossed over from Hollywood to politics at a time when Americans needed to see their men as more than just masculine; they wanted them to be hypermasculine. "Republicans utilize this masculine imagery in national politics to gain voters' trust in times of fear and insecurity," says *Gender & Society*. Add to that Schwarzenegger's self-mocking tone in films such as *Kindergarten Cop* and *Twins*, which allowed us to see his compassionate side, and you had the perfect candidate.

Get involved. If you feel passionately about party politics, there is no reason you can't get involved as a volunteer, helping to raise funds or awareness for the party or helping out in the next election campaign. Go to GOP.com and Democrats.org for more information on the two main political parties. Or if you are so inclined, run for office in your local government.

Politicians as Celebrities

It's not just that celebrities are being used to bolster political campaigns—in an increasingly celebrity-driven world, politicians must cross the line and become entertainers, too. If I say, "Clinton plays the saxophone," I bet you immediately think of

Bill Clinton, who famously jammed the tenor sax at one of his inaugural balls. (If you think of George Clinton of the P-Funk All Stars, an actual musician, then you rock.) This blurring of the line between politics and entertainment is a very unique and modern phenomenon. Can you picture George Washington blowing sax? At least John Quincy Adams actually played the flute, but I'm guessing after helping to create the Monroe Doctrine he did not wow his constituents with a wicked flute solo.

During the 2008 presidential primaries, Barack Obama couldn't just get by on his health care platform, he had to be seen doing that clumsy little dance with Ellen DeGeneres on her show. In the same campaign cycle, the Clintons, Obama, and John McCain appeared (separately) on *Saturday Night Live*. Candidates Mike Huckabee, McCain, and Dennis Kucinich also appeared on *The Daily Show* and *The Colbert Report*—Kucinich even did a whole skit with Colbert.

Apparently it's no longer enough that politicians know how to govern—they also need to know how to entertain and be as appealing as celebrities. Along with that Ivy League education and years of public service, you're gonna need media training, a personal trainer, a publicist, and image consultants.

This politicians-as-entertainers trend began in 1960 with the Kennedy-Nixon debates—the first ever to be televised. Nixon, naive about TV, arrived at the studio with a five o'clock shadow, wearing an ill-fitting shirt, and twenty pounds overweight. He refused to wear makeup and as a result looked sallow, sweaty, and tired on camera. Kennedy, who was on steroids for Crohn's Disease at the time, looked tan, thin, young, vibrant, handsome, and all made-up like a cover model using the cameras the way an actor would. Intellectually the two may have been on par, but physically they definitely were not, and it shaped how voters saw them. Voters who listened to the debate on the radio believed Nixon had won it, while TV viewers thought Kennedy was the winner by a large margin.

It's even more intense nowadays. A political insider who asked to remain anonymous told me, "There is definitely a hypervigilance now as to how our candidates should look on camera and in photographs. But just imagine Abraham Lincoln, arguably our greatest president, in HD. He might not have been elected—Stephen Douglas was definitely the better looking of the two."

"Just imagine Abraham Lincoln, arguably our greatest president, in HD. He might not have been elected."

—(POLITICAL INSIDER)

Franklin D. Roosevelt had a very strong media presence at the time of his presidency. His Fireside Chats on the radio were equally as powerful then as the best candidate sparring with Bill Maher on his HBO show now. I would like to think that FDR could have made it today, but many have said that he would struggle in the age of television.

The blurring of politics and entertainment reached a whole new level of confusion when our TV screens became filled with popular shows taking us "inside" the Oval office. While celebrities are open about using their fame to try and change opinion on political issues, TV dramas have the ability to shape our views about politics and government, insidiously, so that we don't even realize it's happening.

In 2003, researchers found that shows such as the NBC drama series *The West Wing* had an impact on the way we view political candidates. In the *Journal of Communication*, they argued that research being done into how political ideas are formed should be extended to include entertainment television. Other studies have found that we are persuaded by television portrayals of political figures in other shows too, such as the 2005 ABC drama series *Commander in Chief* and FOX's *24*.

Rock the Vote

Oprah publicly endorsed Barack Obama in 2008. Bruce Springsteen, Ashton Kutcher, Whoopi Goldberg, and Ben Affleck all stumped for John Kerry in 2004. Benjamin McKenzie, star of Fox's teen drama *The O.C.* (2003–2007), even addressed the Democratic National Convention in Boston in July 2004. At the time, McKenzie was extremely popular among young people—a symbol of young Hollywood.

We all feel the need to identify with other people in order to form ideas and attitudes when it comes to major decisions, such as our own political self-concept. This is especially true for adolescents, who are still trying to develop their own individual identity. Young folks love to join groups and feel a part of something; it helps them decide what kind of adult they will become and it answers questions as to who they are now. A lot of young people—mostly young girls—identified with McKenzie, or at least his character, "Ryan," and the *O.C.* hunk's involvement in the campaign was no doubt aimed at encouraging them to vote for Kerry.

Oh, and for you fellas out there, you were covered as well: Curt Schilling, a pitcher with the Boston Red Sox, let us know that we should vote for Bush and then won the World Series that year to put an exclamation point at the end of his words.

Just because you played the president in a film, doesn't make you an expert in political science.

On the other side of the aisle, sexy innocent Natalie Portman appeared on Jon Stewart's *The Daily Show* in 2004 wearing a provocative black tank top with the words "Kerry Me" in small white letters on the front of her shirt. A subtle reminder to vote . . . or to look at her chest—either way it had an impact.

While it doesn't seem that celebrity affiliations really helped Kerry in the 2004 election, there is evidence that the efforts of his celebrity advocates did increase voter turnout, especially among American youth (youth voter turnout trended even higher for the 2008 election). McKenzie and Portman were part of a celebrity crew—along with Sean "P. Diddy" Combs, who ran a "Vote or Die" campaign, and myriad celebrity endorsers of "Rock the Vote"—encouraging young people to go out and vote. And according to MTV.com, it worked. They and the Youth Vote Coalition had set a goal of getting 20 million eighteen- to thirty-year-olds to the polls, and in an article that ran after the election, titled "Twenty Million Loud and Then Some: Young People Storm the

Polls," they declared that the goal had been surpassed. In fact 20.9 million young people voted on Election Day 2004, according to the nonpartisan group Center for Information & Research on Civic Learning and Engagement (CIRCLE). More surprising was that there were just as many conservative young voters as there were Democrats. Abandon your idea that the youth don't vote and that when they do, they vote Democrat. In 2004 more twenty-five-year-olds than seventy-five-year-olds voted, and depending upon which stats you look at, anywhere between 33 percent and 49 percent voted Republican.

The Celebrity Citizen

Should a celebrity have to have personal experience with their chosen platform, such as Michael J. Fox and Muhammad Ali do, before they can earn the right to try and sway public opinion and government policy? Or is it okay for a Backstreet Boy to try and save Appalachia?

It may be appropriate for stars to be politically active when they use their influence responsibly and stump for a candidate who is from their home state or who champions beliefs the star is known for. But it can seem plain arrogant when stars act as though they know as much—if not more than—politicians. Just because you played the president in a film, doesn't make you an expert in political science.

Why can't celebrities leave politics to the politicians, who know more about political theory and comparative government, have studied the intricacies and history of world affairs, and frankly, might be smarter than a celebrity? Setting aside the obvious jokes we all like to make about politicians and our general lack of confidence in their integrity, it's likely they know a lot more than a TV star or pop idol does about governing a country. Think about what it takes to become an actor and then think about what it takes to become a political leader. Not quite the same criteria now, are they?

Years ago, Sarandon was chastised by many media watchdog groups for appearing on CBS's *The Early Show* to, rather than discuss her new made-for-TV movie, filibuster poor unsuspecting Harry Smith about "billions of dollars" that were going to be cut from the veterans benefits budget. It was a toss up as to what was most disturbing to the media groups. For some it was that her allegation seemed unsubstantiated, for others it was her arrogance in claiming that she had valuable information accessible only by her. The real issue is that many folks watching that day would have just taken her word for it and not sought out the truth for themselves. After all, she was Sister Helen in *Dead Man Walking*,

Stay informed on the issues. If you don't feel like going out—or can't go out—to campaign speeches, use the Internet. There isn't a single candidate who doesn't use technology to inform the public of his or her political stances. To stay informed about local, state, and federal government, one of the best resources is USA.gov. Also MTV's RocktheVote.com explains the issues in bite-size nuggets. See what interests you and then keep looking for more information. After you've done your research, make up your own mind.

for which she won an Oscar—surely that means she knows stuff we don't . . . right?

Well, maybe. She has made a point of educating herself on the political underpinnings of many social issues; she has also spent time fund-raising for several nonprofit organizations, bringing in untold amounts of money. She could spend her days shopping at Gucci or lunching at Spago, but instead she heads up several advocacy groups and is a champion for human rights and rallies against AIDS, poverty, and hunger. However, the very idea that she would know more about a bill regarding federal spending than a political leader should at least move you to find out the facts for yourself.

I am not questioning the rights of celebrities to become political advocates. Celebrities are citizens, and they have a right—just like everyone else—to express their opinion. And most celebrities who get involved in political causes do so for sincere and selfless reasons, because they really do care about the issues. Actor and social advocate Mike Farrell says, "Actors, if they choose, can take advantage of the platform and opportunity provided by celebrity and use it for social good. If we identify with, are attracted to, lust after, sympathize with, admire, or just care about someone, that connection can carry over . . . to that person's activities outside the theatrical arena."

No one doubts the sincerity of Reba McEntire or Tom Hanks. These people have strong, unwavering political beliefs, and like anyone with enough money to do so, they have the right to donate their money to whatever political causes they like and support their causes however they want. I'm sure a lot of us who are passionate about a political issue wish that we too had a celebrity's platform so our message could be easily heard. But it's important to remember that each of us *can* contribute; we can make our voices heard.

Vote! A wise man once said, "If you don't vote, you can't complain." Even if you vote solely for the privilege of being able to complain, it's worth it. Voting is one of the most American things you can do, and it's a way to influence your world the way a celebrity might. Your vote is your voice, so use it.

CHAPTER NINE

Success and Nuthin' Less

If there's one thing I know about myself it's that I have never and will never drop the ball when the chips are down. I pride myself on that. The higher the stakes, the happier I am, the better I will be.

ROBERT DOWNEY JR.

How do you measure success? Everyone has his or her own yardstick. My good friend, Kirk, measures it by how many dogs a person has. As a dog lover, I get it. He will say to me, "I met this guy who was *so* rich!" Knowing exactly what he means, I will ask, "How many?" to which he might excitedly reply, "He has not one . . . not two . . . not even four . . . but *seven* Airedales!" In my friend's eyes, the guy is just like Warren Buffet. Other people may look at the size of their house or their bank account as a benchmark of achievement, while others may measure success by the size of their family. "I am rich in children and grandchildren," they might say.

But we're all aware of a whole other level of success: fame. Actors who mesmerize us on the screen, singers who enthrall us with their tunes, athletes with extraordinary strength and agility—to the rest of us with humble talents, they seem specially gifted, amazingly talented, and indeed, many of them truly are. We live in a world that worships success, and for many of us, celebrities are the very embodiment of it. After all, if everyone knows their names and they have millions of admirers, they must be the most successful in their field . . . right?

Well, that is until their TV pilot bombs, their top falls off on the red carpet, their long-awaited album is ridiculed by reviewers, or they're found stumbling around a Hollywood parking lot in their pajamas. As we've seen time and time again, a star who once seemed unassailable can suddenly plummet to Earth, burning up in a fiery ball on reentry into the atmosphere. (And how we love to watch each one burn.)

I wonder: Do the extreme examples of success and failure we see in celebrities affect our own attitudes toward success and even our chances of achieving it? Fame seems too flimsy a foundation to base our own success goals on—but do stars actually have something valuable to teach us about achievement?

Mediocrity Is Not an Option

My last book, *The Cult of Perfection,* was about women who are overachievers. Women for whom good enough is never enough, who need to reach higher and go farther than everyone else. Women like me, who are always doing something, trying to squeeze another achievement onto their résumé, constantly striving harder. Many of us today are feeling the pressure to be successful, and not just run-of-the-mill successful but stellar. A job is not enough—you need a career; you need to be a star in your field. A university degree is not enough—you need two or three. Plus, you need to run a marathon or learn Japanese or write a children's book—something to make you just a touch more interesting than you already are, something to give you an edge. The bar has been raised, and we are all stretching up trying to reach it. If you're not achieving something awesome, it's like, "What's the point?"

The pressure many of us feel to achieve remarkable success has many roots, and I'm not about to pin it solely on our celebrity-obsessed culture. But you have to wonder whether placing those with exceptional talents—gifted actors and singers, amazing sportspeople, impossibly beautiful models—up on a pedestal causes us to continually raise our standards higher, until to be considered truly successful we need to break a world record, win an Oscar, and release our own fragrance line. Okay, you mightn't feel as though you need to go to that extreme, but you may feel that you have to achieve similar success in your own career, be it employee of the month or winning your industry's highest honors. Good enough is no longer good enough.

Focus on what matters. One observation we can make from celebrities who keep their heads and lead a happy, together life (versus those who unravel and end up having to prove to a judge why they should be allowed in a car with their babies) is that they are able to keep things in perspective and focus on the stuff that really matters, such as family, friends, and being part of a community. Stars go off the rails when they cut themselves off from normal life, focus entirely on their careers, or start using alcohol and drugs to deal with the pressures of fame and the stress of paparazzi. Though you may not have a pack of photogs swarming outside your house, you can apply the same principles to dealing with the stresses of ordinary life.

Maybe this immense pressure we feel to keep up—and the disappointment of knowing that we can't—is one of the reasons we love it when celebrities fail. When their movies bomb, their albums are panned, or they have a breakdown and end up in a rehab facility, perhaps it makes us feel a little better. It makes the celebrities more human, more like us. For a moment we recognize the limitations of fame and think, "See, this level of success must be unattainable if [insert your favorite fallen star] can't maintain it." So the pressure's off.

A star is only as good as his or her last smash hit or award, an athlete as invincible as his or her last world record.

In the world of celebrity, though, the pressure is never off. A star is only as good as his or her last smash hit or award, an athlete as invincible as his or her last world record. If a singer is out of the public eye for more than a year, her or she has to release a comeback album. When Academy Award winner Marcia Gay Harden came in to be interviewed one day for my radio show, she had not one, not two, but three movies to promote. She, like most stars now, are juggling multiple big projects.

This is endemic in the whole entertainment industry, which tends to attract overachievers determined to climb their way to the top. Case in point: I interviewed a TV executive who is at the helm of one of the biggest television companies—putting her at the highest level in the television industry. She told me, "I'm the oldest of six children, and from the time I can remember I've felt compelled to be the leader of the pack." Her mother stuck with her abusive father, but as her mother's self-esteem shrunk, "somehow roles of mother and daughter reversed and I found myself taking care of the family. We owned a family restaurant where I worked fourteen hours a day, seven days a week." In her early twenties she left the restaurant and went back to school. "To work my way through college, I had two jobs, both at restaurants, and received employee of the year at one, and had the highest overall sales for the year at the other. I've always believed that whatever you do, do your best." After college, she went for interviews at two film studios and was hired at both the same day. "I knew it was a sign that I was to pursue the field of entertainment, although I knew how competitive and cutthroat it could be. And so here I am, a TV executive, still climbing my way to the top, still supporting family members with no regrets and having the time of my life!"

Did she say, "Still climbing my way to the top"? In most people's eyes, she *is* at the top. I can't imagine where she would go—but her never-ending drive for the next pinnacle of success sums up the attitude of most people in the entertainment industry.

I Play a Doctor in Real Life

Success in your chosen field relies on choosing the right field in the first place. Lousy at English and history but great at math and chemistry? Maybe "scientist" is looking more promising as a

The Footprints of Success

Our relationship with celebrities is especially complicated where attitudes toward success are concerned. For some people, a successful celebrity is a shining example, a role model for all that they can achieve, someone who gives them inspiration to accomplish their goals. But to others, a successful celebrity is nothing more than a reminder of all they haven't achieved, a mirror of their worst fears and an illustration of the fame, glittering triumph, and public adoration they may never enjoy. Surprisingly, whether you are inspired or deterred by the success of stars has a great deal to do with the color of your skin.

Over the past twenty years, and backed up again recently by a study published in the *Journal of Black Psychology*, researchers have found that black people report higher levels of self-esteem than white people. White people, it has been found, tend to base their self-esteem on the approval of others, while black people do not. Also, blacks have a stronger ethnic identity, which plays a big part in their self-esteem.

Studies out of the University of North Carolina concluded that whites' self-esteem tends to be *negatively* affected by the success of their white celebrity counterparts, whereas black people are positively affected by the success of black celebrities—and this goes beyond just the random actor; it includes rappers and sports stars too.

Furthermore, black and Latino people are not influenced by the "the thin ideal," which has been found to have a greater effect on white people than any other race. A young white woman might look at Keira Knightley, decide that the actress is gorgeous and she could never look like her, and have lower self-esteem as a result. Latinas and black girls—who have a stronger ethnic identity and also, according to research, enjoy a different idea of what beauty is—would have a different response. A young black woman, for instance, might look at Beyoncé and think to herself, "If she can do it, so can I."

Having low self-esteem doesn't necessarily mean you won't find success in life, but it does have a big impact on goal-setting behaviors. The *Journal of Vocational Behavior* has confirmed that lower self-esteem can predict unemployment, cynicism, and reduced accomplishment at work, not to mention lower levels of job satisfaction.

In general I'd prefer not to waste my time looking at the razor-thin celebrity ideal and feeling down about myself, although I'm sure in my twenties it was inevitable. Now when things are tough, I think about Snoop Dogg. Many folks like to quote great philosophers like Mark Twain or Winston Churchill. I like to quote the great Snoop Dogg when he says, "Success and nuthin' less." Yes, Snoop, words of wisdom for us all to live by. Those words, in all of their rhythmic splendor, help me barrel through a particularly harsh day. When I'm feeling that I am getting farther away from my goals I, like so many others, think about Snoop Dogg—"Success and nuthin' less"—and I feel better.

career choice than "lawyer." Clueless about biology but excel at art? Perhaps graphic design is a better option than medicine.

"Duh, everyone knows that," I hear you say.

Well, maybe choosing the right career isn't quite so straightforward after all. Young people get scads of information—on jobs, relationships, and everything in between—not just from school guidance counselors or from their parents, but also from television and film. We have all seen the numbers telling us how many hours of TV per day kids watch—lots! But what we see on TV and in film doesn't always mirror the real world, and this is especially problematic for young people watching and identifying with their favorite actors and imagining themselves in their roles.

Kids coming out of college are choosing careers based on the information they glean from television programs.

Regular viewers of *Grey's Anatomy*, *ER*, or *House* may think they know what it's like to be in the operating room— sorry, the "OR"—where scrumptious doctors are only occasionally forced to quit their romantic intrigues and/or backstabbing to dramatically yell "Stat!" or "Clear!" (or, in the case of *House*, rule out sarcoidosis). Those who avidly watch *Law & Order* and *CSI* may feel they know their way around a crime scene or the courtroom as well as any attorney or judge. We get lots of messages about occupations and what it takes to be successful in them from these TV shows. In fact kids coming out of college are choosing careers based on the information they glean from television programs, if they haven't had an internship or seen a real example of what kind of career they want. Don't believe me? Well, I have a study . . .

For three years psychologists at the University of Pennsylvania followed a group of career seekers, who they had asked what it took to be a doctor, psychiatrist, paramedic, judge, lawyer, and police officer. What they found was that those who got their information on those jobs solely from what they saw on television were completely unsuccessful in landing one of those jobs. The other group, who had personal experience, for instance through an internship or a close relative in that profession, had a much easier time, because they understood the work involved and the path they had to take in order to get there. This says that the more realistic a career is to you, the better your odds are of making it happen—in other words, an obsession with Ellen Pompeo doesn't mean you should try to become a doctor.

What else does this say? It says if there is something you always thought you wanted to do, finding a way to experience it firsthand is your best guarantee of success. Any time you see chef Gordon Ramsay on television trying to salvage a restaurant that is about to close its doors because someone thought it would be a "cool idea" to own a restaurant, it's usually because they saw folks such as Ramsay, Mario Batali, or Emeril Lagasse on TV and figured, "Hey, that looks like fun, how hard can it be?" On *Ramsay's Kitchen Nightmares* I have yet to see one chef/owner who has been to culinary school, let alone one that has ever worked in a restaurant prior to owning one. Celebrity chefs are celebrity chefs for a reason. Talent, hard work, and actual sweat went into making them who they are. Unfortunately you don't get to see that part on TV. You only get to see how cute Bobby Flay looks grillin' & chillin'.

Start small. Research your chosen career and what you need to do to get there. Set yourself a clear goal and smaller goals leading up to it; write a list if it helps. If you know that one day you want to be a rodeo clown, first you need to learn how to ride a horse, then you need to go to clown school, and then buy big rubber shoes—but take baby steps, knowing that the journey is the most fun part of it. Often celebrities are nostalgic for the days when they were building their careers—the ease of it. Don't let those moments pass you buy. Savor each and every one of them, but keep your eye on the prize.

What Is Success?

In the world of celebrity, this question seems ridiculously easy to answer. Success is Julia Roberts, Nicole Kidman, George Clooney, Brad Pitt. It's Tiger Woods, Michael Jordan, Tom Brady. It's winning a Grammy, Super Bowl, or a PGA tournament. It's having your star on the Hollywood walk of fame or your picture on the cover of *Time* magazine.

If you think this is what celebrity success is about, and thus is what *all* success can ultimately be measured against, it's time to think again. In your own life, you probably think of success as encompassing a balance of different things: financial security, job fulfillment, a happy family life, health, a group of supportive friends (or in Kirk's case, a wealth of dogs). Apply those standards to the world of celebrity, and suddenly stardom doesn't look like such a worthy benchmark.

Winning an award can ensure you lifelong fame, but does it mean success in the sense of lifelong fulfillment or a steady career? Think of the "Oscar curse" that bygone stars such as Mira Sorvino, Roberto Benigni, Halle Berry, Adrien Brody, and Marisa Tomei have had to endure. Berry, who won in 2002 for *Monster's Ball*, disappointed us in *Die Another Day*, and if that wasn't bad enough, won a Razzie for her atrocious stint as a superhero in *Catwoman*. Tomei's Oscar for *My Cousin Vinny* in 1993 left us wanting more of her comedic talents, but she followed it up with a small part in *Chaplin* and then a series of films unbecoming of an Oscar recipient: *Only You* and *The Perez Family*. The others, too, fell short of our expectations of an Oscar winner. Even Julia Roberts had a series of—let's call them less than successful—movies after her 2000 win for *Erin Brockovich*. She followed that film up with *The*

Success is Julia Roberts, Nicole Kidman, George Clooney, Brad Pitt. It's Tiger Woods, Michael Jordan, Tom Brady. It's winning a Grammy, Super Bowl or a PGA tournament.

Mexican, America's Sweethearts, and *Confessions of a Dangerous Mind*—not bad films, just not what we would expect from someone with an Academy Award.

Define success. The most important thing for your own happiness and satisfaction is deciding what success looks like to *you.* Not what television programs, celebrity weeklies, or celebrity news shows say is a successful life. For some, success might mean earning money, buying a house in a chic neighborhood, or doing graduate studies at Harvard. For others, it might be growing the perfect azalea, having a happy home, or learning how to knit socks. Doesn't matter what it is, so long as it's *your* definition of success that you're living by.

Fame Won't Pay the Rent

Some of the wealthiest people in the entertainment industry are not the ones with their names in lights. My friend Douglas is a Broadway theater actor. He's nobody you would have ever have heard of, but he has steady work. He also does voiceovers—that's when you are watching a commercial and some disembodied voice tells you that odors from bacteria are deep inside your comfy sofa, invading your home so you should use Febreeze Deep Clean to combat said bacteria. He makes a seven-figure yearly salary and just bought a penthouse in an exclusive area of Manhattan's Upper West Side worth $2.5 million. I consider him a success—he probably has more money than Molly Ringwald, and you've heard of her.

Any number of reality-TV or YouTube stars are famous but not rich. Constantine Maroulis, *American Idol* finalist and soap opera actor, told me that he may be more famous than rich: "I make personal appearances because I need that money to do what I want to do, so I sit there and answer questions about *American Idol*. I don't want to do it every day of my life, but I do enjoy meeting fans and hearing where they are from, and they say things like 'We voted for you' or 'We stopped watching when you were voted off.'" In those fans' eyes, he is talented and famous and therefore successful. They, like most people, probably think his success includes financial wealth, but the famous don't always achieve that balance.

The celebrity mentality is to live like a star even if you haven't had a job in two years, and even if your last five films tanked.

There are plenty of well-known actors who are living paycheck to paycheck or worrying that if their show gets canceled they'll be typecast for life and won't have a hope of getting another big role. That seems to have happened to some of the *Seinfeld* folks and to some of the *Friends* cast, too.

Even worse, plenty of celebrities end up broke. Would it surprise you to learn that Burt Reynolds filed for bankruptcy? How about Kim Basinger? More stars than you can imagine have lived beyond their means and ended up with nothing. Basinger had signed on to do the film *Boxing Helena* and during that

same time purchased the town of Braselton, Georgia, for $20 million. When she dropped out of the film, she was sued for breach of contract and had to not only sell the town but file for bankruptcy. The celebrity mentality is to live like a star even if you haven't had a job in two years, and even if your last five films tanked. If you are still famous, well then you must be rich, or on your way back to it, right? And according to the Smoking Gun, which obtained the Florida bankruptcy documents filed by Reynolds, he's $10 million in the hole.

The upper echelons of the Machine—the people whom you've never heard of but create celebrities and hit movies, TV shows, and albums—are the ones who are in perhaps the most enviable position in the entertainment industry. They have power; they can hire and fire celebrities; they make the serious money and have a level of job security that stars never will. You've heard of only a handful of them—Steven Spielberg and Jeffrey Katzenberg, for instance—but lack of fame doesn't mean they are any less successful than big stars.

In the music industry it's the songwriter who makes the real cash, not necessarily the person singing the song. Missy "Misdemeanor" Elliot was rich beyond your wildest dreams before you ever heard of her. She was a highly sought-after songwriter and producer who had written number one hits for several singers, including Aaliyah and Destiny's Child. The same is true for Linda Perry. She fronted a band in the 1990s called 4 Non Blondes that had a hit called "What's Up." A lot of people outside the music business might think of her as a one-hit wonder, because her fame tapered off after that song. What most people don't realize is that her real cash cow is all the hits she has written for everyone from Pink, Gwen Stefani, Alicia Keys, and Christina Aguilera to Celine Dion and the Dixie Chicks. She even spotted the talent of James Blunt early and signed him to her own record label. She's the go-to girl if you want to take a little country out of your western, some gum out of your pop, or add something soft to your rock. Although you may not know her name, she is an astronomical success.

Succeed Like a Star

As so many entertainment-industry insiders have told me, success and fame can be a bit of a lottery. The finest actors, singers, and artists aren't necessarily the ones who make it into the limelight. Though it seems self-evident that the celebrities we know and love were destined to be successful, it took a *lot* of work to claw their way to the top. As they clambered up that golden ladder, competitors were trying to drag them down from below or stomp on their fingers from above. Then when they finally did reach the top—that golden land called "success"—they found that what they were standing on was a razor's edge. One false move—the wrong movie role, bad choice of record label, a drunken indiscretion, a change in public tastes and fashions—and they would be sent crashing down.

It takes a certain kind of person to have the persistence to keep climbing to the top, and then once there, maintain a footing or know how to break his or her fall. What does psychology tell us about these people, the ones who have the determination to just keep going until they reach their goals?

It all comes down to their "personal theory," according to Carol Dweck, one of the first women to truly inspire me in psychology. She says that we each have our own view of the world, a theory that guides us. Your theory informs your beliefs about who is successful and why they are successful. You may believe they got to where they are in their career because they worked hard, or

Live Fast, Die Young

There's another good reason for the musically inclined to opt for a life behind the scenes: Turns out that if living is one of your markers for success, becoming a music star is certainly not a good career option. Researchers at Liverpool John Moores University found that music stars' death risk is two to three times higher than the general population's. The study found that in Britain, those who survived the first twenty-five years of fame ended up returning to the same death risk as normal folk—but sadly, American music stars continued to have high death rates in later life. The study said the difference "might be explained by differences in longer-term experience of fame, with more performing in later years . . . continued media interest and associated stress and substance abuse in North American pop stars." Perhaps most interesting of all, "many [U.S. musicians] die in poverty [since] there is not the same type of public health provision there [as in Britain]."

you may think it's because they were lucky. And that influences the way you approach *your* goals—you are either determined to work hard or to wait for your lucky day. Luck has helped launch many people to stardom, but the stars who endure know that without hard work, their careers will peter out.

Dweck believes that another important factor is your theory about intelligence. Some people believe that intelligence is an unchangeable, fixed kinda thing, where you are stuck with what you were born with, like your height or eye color. But others of us think that we can develop our intelligence. The reason this is so important is that it influences how you will go about achieving your own success. According to Dweck even when people have equal intellectual ability, their theories of intelligence shape their outcomes. If you think that you can do nothing to improve your abilities, you may be more likely to give up in the face of failure, thinking, "I'm just not smart enough." Those who think that intelligence can grow are more likely to take a more challenging path, do whatever they can do, and go wherever the journey takes them, because they believe it is just as important as the outcome. They believe that learning something or putting in a great effort is a success all its own. You've heard of so-called "overnight" celebrity successes that took ten years. These are people who never gave up, despite the unrelenting amount of failure they endured.

There is nothing quite so spectacular as a celebrity's failure. At least if you slip up at work or in your personal life, you won't find the evidence splashed all over the front cover of the next *Us Weekly*. The odd thing about failure is that for some people, it's a motivation to work harder, a mere setback but not the end of the world. For others, it marks the end of an era, a time to move on. If a celebrity spends twelve months making a megabudget Hollywood movie that bombs at the box office, he or she could see it as encouragement to make a better film next time. Or his or her response could be a three-step process: Step one: Fall into depression. Step two: Eat copious amounts of Chunky Monkey ice

> "A common 'solution' might be self-medication . . . leading to poorer and poorer results. Something like this might apply to the Britney Spearses and Amy Winehouses of the world."
>
> —JASON PLAKS, ASSOCIATE PROFESSOR, UNIVERSITY OF TORONTO

cream. Step three: Die. Whether a person bounces back from failure depends on his or her theory about him- or herself. Those who survive and succeed know that when they fail, it's time to learn a new strategy.

Again, it also comes down to whether a person has a fixed mind set or a more flexible viewpoint regarding success and failure. Many celebrities are told from childhood onward "that they have natural, God-given talent," says Jason Plaks, an associate professor at the University of Toronto. If the star has a fixed mind set and "buys into this view of talent—'either you got it or you don't'—then the first time he or she encounters failure should be particularly devastating. . . . On the other hand, someone who perceives his or her effort as a combination of both 'native talent' *and* dynamic factors like effort, strategy, and even luck would be better positioned psychologically to handle [failure]."

Plaks goes on to say that when celebrities with the more rigid idea of talent and success are under pressure—say, from agents and recording labels—"a common 'solution' might be self-medication, which then further impairs [their] work ethic and performance, leading to poorer and poorer results. Something like this might apply to the Britney Spearses and Amy Winehouses of the world.

"Celebrities with a fixed perspective are likely more concerned with what people think of them. These are the people who obsessively track their Google hits and enter their own fan club chatrooms under pseudonyms," notes Plaks. Stars who are more flexible in their thinking "are more concerned with actually putting out the best possible product and continually growing and developing their skills. They are not afraid to take risks and not afraid to fail."

There are sad cases where stars fell from grace and never recovered, but there are also plenty of examples of stars who hit rock bottom but gathered their strength, healed, re-created themselves, and came back even better than before. After the success of *Lois & Clark* in the 1990s, Teri Hatcher sunk into obscurity, barring a few Radio Shack commercials, but then reemerged and carved out an even more successful role as a Desperate Housewife. Daryl Hannah, after falling for Tom Hanks as a fish in *Splash!*, had a long swim back until *Kill Bill*. The stars who make a comeback can end up holding a special place in our thoughts, because they show us how strong the human spirit is. They show us that if we fall, we too can get back up again, head held high, and start afresh.

"The people who have the biggest chance of making a comeback are the ones who didn't go out on bad terms with us, the ones who faded away or self-destructed and we feel sorry for them," says Jarett Weiselman, pop culture expert. "Everyone likes a comeback story because everyone, on some level, hopes to be resilient like that in their own lives—they can triumph over the odds; they can get fired and be near bankruptcy but still come back and make a statement."

Learn by example. In celebrity land, the key to succeeding despite the odds or rising from the ashes of failure seems to be a flexible attitude, greater emphasis on achieving the best you can rather than being strictly concerned about what others think of you, a desire to develop your skills, and the ability to see failure as an opportunity to learn a new strategy. The stars who make it, the stars who weather humiliating failures, the stars who keep a grip on their sanity seem to be the ones who are resilient people with a strong sense of self and the *Terminator* gene that makes them keep working harder and trying to be better all the time.

It's rare that I would suggest looking toward celebrities as role models, but they do make very public examples of the diverse ways of coping with failure, and you can learn from that. Everyone has to face setbacks in life; it's just part of the human condition. Things don't always go the way you'd like, and sometimes you make mistakes. What matters is your attitude and what steps you take next. Do you see failure as the end, or do you have a more optimistic outlook and find the opportunity in the situation? Stars who fail in the most humiliating of ways but regroup and return even stronger than before can be your inspiration.

CHAPTER TEN

And Who Greenlights This Marriage?

I've always had really low self-esteem, and I still do. What's weird about that is being onstage, and the love that you get, and the adoration that you feel from your real fans. It's hard for a partner to compete . . .

MARIAH CAREY

My husband's name is Sean. I tell you this because I am hoping some clever sort out there will help me come up with a catchy way to combine our names, like "Brangelina" and "TomKat." I lament the cleverly monikered yet short-lived "Vaugniston." And I secretly hope to be half of "Deppence" one day, or perhaps if Christian Bale wouldn't mind, we could be "Chrisper."

Then again, some of the seemingly more healthy relationships in Hollywood don't have that one-name dual-person identity: There is no "DemiKut" or "Hankson." So maybe being just "Sean" and "Cooper" is okay, too.

The trend in recent years to fuse the names of star couples seems almost symbolic of what the celebrity relationship represents: a fusing of fame, beauty, and power. It's a cross-fertilization of stardom and prestige. It's the latest romantic-comedy leading man and leading lady hooking up, pop stars melding their celebrity brands together, sports heroes bonding with models (models being the one thing that never goes out of fashion in the celebrity hookup department). Stars almost never wed or shack up with ordinary folk, and this only reinforces the "us and them" aspect of our relationship with celebrities. Us down here and them up there on Mount Olympus—sorry, I mean the Hollywood Hills.

> "She's gorgeous, successful and has got the gorgeous husband, the great career, and one of the best bodies in Hollywood—this can't be fair."
>
> —JARETT WEISELMAN, POP CULTURE EXPERT

We have a voracious appetite for pictures of their fairy-tale weddings in private castles in Scotland with budgets way bigger than what most people pay for their houses. We listen avidly to breathless breaking news reports on which hunky and pert costars have just got together or cheated on each other, which star has stormed out of the couple's home via Harley-Davidson, or who's just had to pony up $150 million in a divorce settlement.

It is no great shock to us—and often has far more entertainment value—when the fairy-tale

Hollywood romance turns into a nightmare of child custody disputes, substance abuse, vicious recriminations, sex tapes, and kooky behavior. Because of their fame and power, we expect celebrities to be dysfunctional and self-absorbed to a degree. We're usually more surprised when their relationships *work* than when they unravel publicly on *Entertainment Tonight* and *TMZ*—but what does that, and our insatiable craving for celeb relationship gossip, say about us?

The Joy of the Ex

To explain the attention we give to the love lives of celebrities, pop culture expert Jarett Weiselman points to the story of Jennifer Aniston and her divorce from Brad Pitt. "The reason we tuned in is because it all seemed too perfect, and *completely unfair!* She's gorgeous, successful and has got the gorgeous husband, the great career, and one of the best bodies in Hollywood—this can't be fair—so when the whole thing fell apart it made sense to everyone who had thought 'I knew it couldn't all be that perfect.' We know there are peaks and valleys in life, but with celebrities we wait for the valley."

Actress Fran Drescher brought her long-term relationship with a much younger hunk to the small screen with her 2005–2006 series *Living with Fran.* I asked her why there is so much in the news about who is dating whom. "I think media tends to cater to the lowest common denominator of readership or viewership. I don't think thinking people care all that much. It's a shame because I believe that most people would take just as much pleasure in learning about altruistic people doing meaningful things in all different walks of life."

Weiselman disagrees: "Unfortunately sex and scandal sells. Humanitarian efforts may sell copies of *Time* magazine, but they are not going to sell a gossip magazine or a celebrity weekly."

Perhaps one reason why we like to follow the highs and lows of stars' romances is that it's a way to live vicariously through them, indulging in a fantasy of the life we could have if we were celebs. (Hey, it wouldn't matter if your relationship with Jake Gyllenhaal stalled—if you were a celebrity you could move on to, I don't know, Adrian Grenier or someone.)

And we enjoy it when stars' relationships crumble because the world makes sense to us again. It brings the stars back down to a more human level, and a comforting thought passes through our minds: "Maybe I didn't have a diamond-encrusted one-off wedding gown personally designed by Vera Wang or Carolina Herrera, or a ceremony in a medieval European cathedral, but at least my marriage lasted."

"I think media tends to cater to the lowest common denominator of readership or viewership."

—FRAN DRESCHER

Love-Life Archetypes

Celebrities' love lives are not unique. As Drescher reminds me, "Although celebrities lives are focused more in media for the most part, pain, love, death, and

loss are universal." Over and over again you see that celebrities have the same types of relationships and relationship problems as we have, but theirs are on a more spectacular and public scale. In fact we can look at celebrities' relationships as larger-than-life archetypes of all relationships.

In It for the Short Haul

Pamela Anderson is famous for short, spontaneous marriages to entertainment industry bad boys—such as Tommy Lee, whom she married after knowing him for ninety-six hours, or Kid Rock whom she married and divorced soon after, and then Rick Salomon, whom she reportedly divorced two months after their wedding. Pammie is not alone; many celebrities are famous for marrying impulsively and for short durations.

Britney Spears had a fifty-five-hour marriage to her childhood friend Jason Alexander, then married Kevin Federline after knowing him for only three months. We have accepted that Drew Barrymore just does not do lengthy marriages and neither does Carmen Electra. She was briefly married to Dennis Rodman after dating him for about four months, then had a short-lived marriage to musician Dave Navarro.

In celebrity land, quick, impulsive marriages have been taking place for decades: In 1964 when Ethel Merman announced her marriage to Ernest Borgnine—which lasted only thirty-two days and is immortalized in her autobiography with a blank page—she had tongues wagging all over the country. Merman and Borgnine's marriage epitomized the image the public had, and still has, of celebrities: They are impulsive, unrealistic, dramatic and behave differently than normal people do.

Before you roll your eyes at the next ill-advised celebrity

quickie marriage, though, think about this: Turns out that we aren't too far behind.

Stacy Schneider, a former divorce attorney and the author of *He Had It Coming: How to Outsmart Your Husband and Win Your Divorce*, says that she saw quickie marriages in her practice all the time, mostly among younger couples. "The new generation of those getting married seem to end up becoming 'quickie marriages' because we have no-fault divorce, where you can sail through the divorce process. I have seen so many marriages that last no longer than a year; some of them came to me and they were still sending out 'thank you' notes from the wedding."

"I have seen so many marriages that last no longer than a year; some of them . . . were still sending out 'thank you' notes from the wedding."

—STACY SCHNEIDER, AUTHOR OF *HE HAD IT COMING*

Another factor in the short-term-marriage trend is that the stigma of being a divorcée is gone. Schneider says, "Being divorced is nothing to be embarrassed about anymore. As a matter of fact, in the dating world it can be a plus to be divorced. You meet a guy and he doesn't feel as though you are desperate and sizing him up for marriage."

She notes that many of the younger couples coming to her for divorces after short marriages had known each other for only a short time before their wedding—just like many of the celebrity quickie-marriage offenders.

Ted Huston, professor of human ecology and psychology at the University of Texas, spent fifteen years studying the relationship between the length of time a couple spends dating and their marital success. He found that, on average, a happy and successful couple dates for two years and four months before getting married. If you marry sooner than that, your marriage probably won't be well grounded, because the reason you fell in love quickly is that you idealized your partner, perhaps seeing him as the perfect Prince Charming, rather than getting to know him in all his complexity, both the positive and negative aspects.

On average, a happy and successful couple dates for two years and four months before getting married.

The Serial Bride or Groom

With such a high divorce rate, having more than one marriage in a lifetime is hardly unique—but for celebrities it's almost *mandatory* to have several marriages under their belt before they reach for that AARP card. It all begins with the obscure pre-fame marriage to a gas station owner's son

Pretty Reformed Woman

Celebrity relationships can show us that there is hope for all those who tend to rush headlong into committed relationships. Just look at Julia Roberts.

Short-haul star brides such as Anderson and Electra come across as flashy and showy larger-than-life women, so we aren't that shocked by their rapid turnover of marriages. Roberts, on the other hand, surprised us. In the 1990s she was on the cover of everything and was relentlessly pursued by the paparazzi. And with her serial romances, she didn't disappoint. After a multitude of engagements and a slew of very public relationships to high-profile men—Dylan McDermott, Kiefer Sutherland, Liam Neeson, Daniel Day-Lewis, Jason Patric, Benjamin Bratt, and Matthew Perry—she finally married Lyle Lovett, after knowing him for just three weeks. She divorced him a year or so later. But as the new millennium approached, she settled down with cameraman Danny Moder and forged a relationship that her fans deemed worthy of her Oscar-winning status.

or a waitress, then they trade up to other celebrities. In addition, there are a few called-off engagements and a few marriages to a string of glamorous people who are each seemingly "the One."

Elizabeth Taylor certainly has not married other stars exclusively. Who can forget the construction worker, Larry Fortensky? But she has got to be the gold-standard celebrity serial bride. Before she hit sixty, she had racked up a phenomenal eight marriages. And she represents a subset of the celebrity serial bride or groom—those who get divorced and remarry the same spouse again, in her case Richard Burton. Lana Turner had eight husbands and also belonged to the "I married the same man twice" club—for her it was Stephen Crane. Film producer, actor, and writer Robert Evans has been married seven times (and was rumored to have had a dalliance with Lana Turner, among others). Zsa Zsa Gabor has had nine husbands.

Some of today's stars are doing their bit to uphold this grand celebrity tradition. Billy Bob Thornton has had five wives, and Geena Davis five husbands. J Lo was on her third husband by the tender age of thirty-four, plus let's not forget the whole "Bennifer" engagement interlude.

In 1999 the *Journal of Divorce and Remarriage* showed that people who remarry following a divorce have a greater risk of a subsequent divorce than those marrying for the first time. Meaning once you are on that train, you are likely to ride those

Billy Bob Thornton has had five wives, and Geena Davis five husbands. J Lo was on her third husband by the tender age of thirty-four.

rails again and again. However, remarriage seems to be better for kids than remaining a single parent after a divorce. Not only does the second income help, but kids from a home with a remarried parent academically outperform students who live with one divorced parent.

What makes people remarry goes back to how they learned to attach to others during early childhood. The *Journal of Divorce and Remarriage* published another study that found "multiple marriers are more likely to be avoidantly attached," that is, they are more likely to be fiercely independent, show little distress at being alone, and are in their element when they are off doing things on their own. Someone like that sounds perfectly suited to a life of fame and celebrity, so I guess it's little wonder that celebrities are so well-known for their staggering marriage tallies.

The Showmance

I constantly hear celebrities describe the cast and crew of their TV show or film sets as "like a family." They always say that, "We are like family." Well, it's a weird incestuous one when you start dating the guy playing your brother, and it often happens that costars soon become romantically linked. When you spend most of your day on a TV or movie set, how could you not carry it over into your personal life, especially if there's a benefit to your career? *Mr. and Mrs. Smith* became a much more intriguing film when rumors began to fly that Brad and Angelina were real-life lovers (rumors that she substantiated in 2008), especially since he was still married to Jennifer Aniston. Brad and Angelina's bond turned out to be a serious one that was to endure long after their movie—but other stars have come together for career-boosting (and sometimes even rumored to be contractual) "showmances."

Don't do it just because *they* do. Does constant exposure to nightmare celebrity relationships lower our own relationship standards? "The issue here is that celebrities are treated in our society as modern-day religious icons," says psychologist James Houran, Ph.D. "When we see successful and respected celebrities engaged in disposable relationships, it gives everyday people inherent permission, and even justification, for following suit. The idea is, "If they do it, then it must be okay for anyone to do it." Resist falling into this kind of thinking. Don't look to Hollywood to justify your romantic choices: That validation will be hollow and unsatisfying.

The showmance is the mirage of a real relationship for the benefit of the press, and it can take many forms. There are the actors who hook up for a short period; that is, long enough to promote a movie they both star in. There are the stars who trade up: B-listers borrowing a little of their partners' A-list dazzle. And there is endless speculation that a whole pantheon of gay male Hollywood stars still believe it's 1950 and need to marry a gorgeous woman, and maybe even have babies, to keep getting those leading-man roles. All these different showmances share one thing in common: While the relationship remains mutually beneficial, the couple stays together, but as soon as the front is no longer necessary, the relationship fades away.

At first you might think the showmance doesn't exist in the real world, but look at the trophy-wife phenomenon or any other relationship people enter into simply for social status or financial security—or even, to this day, to cover up homosexuality or gender-identity issues. Celebrity showmances meet their demise when they have performed their PR function, and from this we can take a lesson for our own lives: Relationships based not on genuine affection and shared goals, but rather on bling, prestige, and make-believe have no solid foundation. They're simply not built to last.

Celebrity showmances meet their demise when they have performed their PR function.

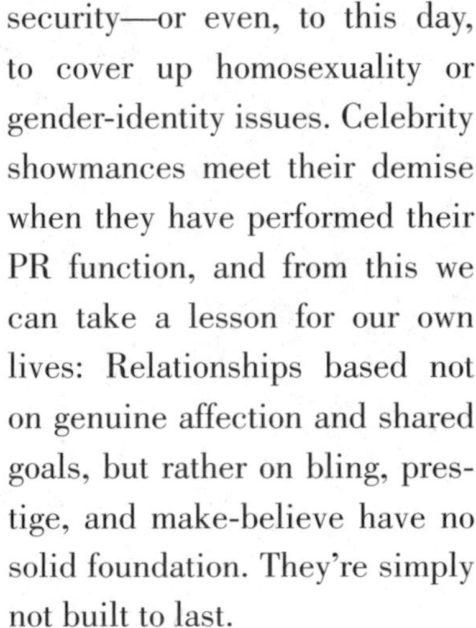

The Confirmed Bachelor

Stars such as Matthew McConaughey, Leonardo DiCaprio, Orlando Bloom, and Justin Timberlake have spent their peak celebrity years unmarried and seem to be in no hurry to settle down. But earning the title of "confirmed bachelor" comes down to more a state of mind than matrimony, for this category also includes a number of stars who did at one time walk down the aisle. Think of Colin Farrell, who was married to the mother of his son for about four months. George Clooney was married once, but he has publicly sworn (much to many women's great disappointment) that he will never marry again nor have children.

Solid Star Couples

Hovering beneath the radar is a relatively small but impressive bunch of celebrities who are in a lasting relationship. You don't hear much about their private lives, because they keep them just that—private—and they don't do the stuff that gets your mug shot on every celebrity gossip Web site. I do not dare to even whisper the names of these couples, for fear that I will in some way jinx them. But perhaps the lesson we can take from them and apply to our own lives is this: They focus on nurturing their relationships and families above all else, and they value time with the ones they love over constant fame and attention.

To some men in the real world, it may look as if these bachelor stars have the perfect life. With their good looks, charm, and status, they can date an infinite array of hot actresses, songstresses, and supermodels. It's like they're at a Chinese restaurant with the biggest lazy Susan imaginable. "I've tried the lingerie model. Hmm, I think I'll have a nubile young actress—then again, that pop star with the new number one hit looks tasty."

Many a woman has been spurred on by an emotionally unavailable, never-quite-ready-to-settle-down guy, thinking she'll be the one who finally breaks or tames him. But even if by some miracle he happens to look like Clooney, pursuing a man who can be committed only to bachelorhood usually ends in heartbreak.

It seems sexy, mysterious, and attractively elusive when a male celebrity stays single well into adulthood, but in ordinary life it is problematic. In 2000, Iowa State University published a paper that referred to the adult bachelors (and bachelorettes) of the world as "gender transgressors," in that by staying single into adulthood they have defied what we deem appropriate for gender identity. Society says that at a certain age men and women should be paired off, period. Anything that deviates is . . . well, deviant.

This is one area of human relationships where there is a double standard: one rule for celebrities, another for us. It's okay for Mick Jagger to be unmarried in his sixties, but if your child's pediatrician is in his sixties and still unmarried, it makes you uncomfortable. "What's wrong with him?" you think to yourself.

December-May

One of the most oft-recurring and recognizable celebrity relationship patterns is the older, established male star and his lovely, young up-and-coming bride. But plenty of female stars are now turning the tables, most notably Demi Moore and Ashton Kutcher, and Mariah Carey and Nick Cannon. There is a growing trend toward December-May relationships among celebrities and the rest of society, too.

The more familiar May-December romances are not as scandalous as the December-May ones. A woman coupled with a man who is younger, much younger, flies in the face of all we know about evolution and biology. According to the rules of those sciences, it makes sense that a younger, more fertile, attractive woman would seek an older, more financially stable male to attend to her offspring's needs—which in nonpsychology speak means you get a rich older guy to send your kids to college and buy them their first BMW at sixteen.

According to the journal *Current Anthropology*, we need to forget about evolution and biology when looking for an explanation for these relationships. It isn't a reproductive strategy, it's a social preference. A younger man is a status symbol in some circles, just as the new bag from Balenciaga or the latest Jimmy Choo boot might be. The increasing number of December-May relationships is a direct result of women's ability to succeed at all levels of business, as they take the mantles of CFOs, presidents, and captains of industry once reserved for men. Younger boyfriends or spouses are the spoils of those achievements.

Cut to the entertainment industry and the astronomical salaries of actresses, female pop stars, and women who are now running film studios. With money and success come personal trainers, fabulous vacations when they can take them, noninvasive surgical procedures such as Botox so they look great for their younger beaus, and access to health professionals and preventive medicine so they can keep working at the pace of women half their age. The same way that rich, powerful men always enjoyed the bonus of a young hot starlet on their arm, older women can accessorize with a younger model (literally and figuratively).

And December-May can be a recipe for a successful pairing. A 2003 study conducted by AARP of over 3,500 singles revealed that 34 percent of all women over the age of forty were happily dating younger men, and 35 percent preferred it to dating older men. Go cougars!

The Happily Unmarried

The U.S. Census Bureau reported in 2001 that of the 72.5 million children under the age of eighteen, 3 percent (2.1 million) lived with their unmarried Tim Robbins and Susan Sarandon–like

Maintain a great friendship. I often wonder how good a celebrity married couple's friendship can be when the two are working on films or on tour in different countries for months at a time. The key to a solid foundation in any healthy marriage is to have a strong bond as friends above all else. Be glad that your significant other is your best friend and you don't have to share him or her with the hot new young actress or actor as they shoot a love scene in Paris while you stay home.

parents. By 2006, an estimated 54 percent of the adult population was unmarried, a figure that was up dramatically over the past twenty years. It seems that in this regard, celebrities are mirroring a trend already happening in society. Our attitudes and lives have changed to the degree that when we watched the reality show, *Gene Simmons Family Jewels*, we weren't at all shocked that he and Shannon Tweed have been happily unmarried with children for years. (The only shocking part was when Simmons acquiesced to plastic surgery.)

Australian scholar and writer dale spender (who doesn't use caps in her name . . . long story, Google it) has written prolifically on the subject of marriage and parenting, and offers this idea to explain why increasing numbers of couples are remaining unmarried, even when they have children: "Many women may not want to be wives, but most eventually do want to be mothers."

Reality TV Marriages

One type of celebrity couple the tabloids have trouble speculating about is the married celebrity couple with a reality TV show. These couples want to show us *everything*. It's less a case of "Will you take this man . . ." and more a case of TV producers rubbing their hands together and saying, "This'll make a great reality show."

Inevitably the relationship ends soon after the ratings tank. Who can forget Jessica Simpson and Nick Lachey as the *Newlyweds*? Or Britney Spears and Kevin Federline in the aptly named *Chaotic*, which lasted a whole five episodes? Then there's Hulk Hogan and his ex-wife Linda, Whitney Houston and Bobby Brown, and Carmen Electra and Dave Navarro. Even Liza Minnelli and David Gest reportedly had a reality TV show in the works, but I guess the marriage didn't last long enough to get a camera crew together. And let's take a moment to remember those reality TV relationship pioneers, the *Bachelors* and *Bachelorettes*, whose relationships have mostly ended up on the scrapheap. (Trista and Ryan Sutter, who not only managed to wed but also start a family, are notable exceptions.)

Psychologist James Houran, Ph.D., is a relationship expert, co-author of *Celebrity Worshippers: Inside the Minds of Stargazers*, and a noted authority on celebrity worship. He says that while the impact of reality TV programming on celebrity relationships hasn't really been studied, celebrity couples live their lives as if they are in "a daily reality TV show" anyway.

I interviewed Kevin Federline on my radio show on Halloween 2006, when he came on to talk about the release of his CD *Playing with Fire*. It was at a significant time in the entertainer's life, not long after *Chaotic* and just days before his acrimonious breakup with Britney Spears. It seemed that his attitude to the intrusion of the media into the couple's life had changed since he'd agreed to share his home movies with the world in a reality TV show. It had certainly made him aware of how much disruption media exposure can cause to family life.

By this point, Spears had given birth to their second baby, Jayden James, and Federline had had time to get used to living in the media bubble that was his then-wife's universe. The stories in the media about the couple were getting so outlandish that I wondered whether the two might have started some of them as a joke. "We don't do any of that," he replied. "It's crazy. That's how much attention the media gives us. They make up all this stuff; we don't have to do anything."

He went on to talk of his concerns about having the media following his children's lives. "It's overwhelming and kind of a curse, and as a father and a parent I really don't like my children being out there the way that they are, but at the same time there's nothing you can really do about it. [And] you don't want to make the fans feel like you are jaded; you want to give them what they want. But I mean, it's a fine line when you are dealing with family and private life."

It's unlikely that a TV producer is going to call you tomorrow and ask you and your family to star in a new reality show. But this relationship archetype can still apply to your life. There are couples whose relationships suffer because there are too many eyes watching their every move, and they receive too many brutally honest reviews of their performance. There are new parents who need a bit of support but instead have in-laws who watch and criticize their every parenting choice. There are couples who have friends and family who peer over their shoulders and try to steer the relationship.

Be thankful you aren't a celebrity. You and your significant other do not have the paparazzi following your every move; you do not live with the threat of your TV show being canceled; you don't wake in the morning worried if today is your day for a tabloid scandal. Living a normal life is a gift to a marriage. You get to define your relationship, no one does it for you. Problems arise for a celebrity couple when they don't have enough real couple time. "Without privacy and psychological space, a couple has little chance to build a strong, loving, and enduring couple identity," says psychologist James Houran. "That is, the couple no longer has that relationship as a retreat or a sanctuary from business and other pressures." Make the most of your noncelebrity status and find private time as a couple so you can create the relationship that you both want.

While your small circle may judge you, the entire world judges celebrities after seeing only the edited-down version of their lives, which often includes only their darkest and most embarrassing moments. The tragedy is when, through celeb-reality television, we get to watch someone completely deteriorate, such as Anna Nicole Smith, whose reality TV show was a harbinger of things to come.

The Tragic Bride

Nobody knows the Anna Nicole Smith story better than Rita Cosby, award-winning TV host and author of the *New York Times*–bestselling book *Blonde Ambition: The Untold Story Behind Anna Nicole Smith's Death.*

Cosby says, "Anna Nicole Smith was always looking for real love, acceptance, and certainly fame. She desperately craved and thrived in the limelight, far beyond being a *Playboy* cover girl." Smith's story is incredibly tragic, from her rise to fame as a *Playboy* and Guess model to her descent into substance abuse, which eventually took her life at the age of thirty-nine.

"Her tireless battle to gain validation and acceptance in a world surrounded by swirling media headlines also caused her life to spiral downward, as she sought comfort with countless prescription drugs to numb the reality that had enveloped her life," says Cosby. "Although to the world she projected an air of star-like confidence, she also had a needy and childlike spirit, and was crumbling behind closed doors."

Perhaps even more than her drug problem, she was known for her relationships with men—perhaps another way she sought security. She was married at the age of seventeen to the father of her first child, Daniel; the couple separated within two years. Just as her career was beginning to take off, she met billionaire J. Howard Marshall II, a customer at a strip club where she was performing. He was eighty-nine and she merely twenty-six. After the couple married, Smith would never escape the claim that she was a gold digger, though she would deny it to the end. That pairing produced the bizarre and unforgettable image of Smith at Marshall's funeral, all glammed up and wearing her wedding dress.

Her relationships continued to get even stranger, with her ceremonial but not legally binding wedding to her lawyer Howard K. Stern shortly after the birth of her second child (fathered by another man) and the methadone-related death of her son, Daniel.

How did Anna Nicole seemingly lose control of her own life? Cosby cautions, "Celebrities must remember fame is fleeting. The same media that builds you up will also often be there to report your shortcomings, especially when you have entered the voracious tabloid world."

Only Smith would ever know the real reasons behind her marriages and liaisons with men, but toward the end it seemed that her complicated relationships reflected her internal chaos, which the constant media attention only provoked and intensified.

Can Two Egos Share One Relationship?

The future of our society can look quite grim when you view it through the prism of celebrity relationship disasters. It may appear that no one respects marriage or committed relationships anymore. But don't despair. While the state of celebrity relationships in some ways mirrors changes in society as a whole, we must not forget that celebrity couples have some unique characteristics that add to their risk of relationship failure.

Recent research into celebrity narcissism reveals something profound that explains not only their relationship challenges but some of their diva-like behavior as well.

On ABC's *20/20*, Dr. Robert Millman of Cornell's Weill Medical College, explained a psychological syndrome he was the first to identify, called "acquired situational narcissism." Narcissism—a personality disorder characterized by having little empathy for others and a grandiose sense of importance—was traditionally thought to begin only in childhood. That was until Millman began seeing patients who had acquired it later in life, after they had become enormously successful.

Acquired situational narcissism affects not only famous entertainers but also politicians, billionaires, renowned authors—anyone who has gained a degree of success, fame, or notoriety. When a person reaches the status of a celebrity, according to Millman, it can lead to narcissism and behavior that borders on unspeakable, antisocial, and sometimes angry. On *20/20*, ABC used the example of Alec Baldwin's abusive cell phone tirade to his young daughter in 2007. Millman told ABC that a narcissistic celebrity's outrageous sense of entitlement can be accompanied by anger: "It's this huge rage that you're not as great as you could be, or you're not being perceived as great as you could be."

If you think you are better than everyone else (including your partner), regularly take advantage of others, need to be admired at all times, and lack empathy, how can you expect to have good relationships? Clearly if celebrities succumb to acquired situational narcissism, they will struggle to have successful and healthy relationships.

"Many celebrities have the resources to indulge their impulses with little to no regard for negative consequences."

—PSYCHOLOGIST JAMES HOURAN, PH.D.

And it's not only acquired narcissism that afflicts celebrities and dooms many of their relationships. Dr. Drew Pinsky and his colleague Mark Young have also noted that a career in the public eye attracts those who were *already* higher in the trait of narcissism.

A career in the spotlight is also often chosen by those with personalities high in impulsivity, which accounts for their ability to drop everything and fly to a location half way around the world at a moment's notice. Impulsivity can be beneficial for stars' careers—for their relationships, not so much.

Psychologist James Houran, Ph.D., has studied star couples and their likelihood of relationship success and says, "It's important to note that celebrities can impulsively *enter* or impulsively *leave* relationships.

"Many celebrities have the resources to indulge their impulses with little to no regard for negative consequences. Money and insulation by an entourage can minimize negative effects that often follow from impulsive decisions made by everyday people. In fact, good PR agents can turn impulsive acts into positive buzz for a celebrity."

> "Sex and money are the two leading causes of relationship breakups."
>
> —PSYCHOLOGIST JAMES HOURAN, PH.D.

For actors, another key issue that endangers their relationships is performing in romantic scenes. "Constantly filming love scenes does not really help relieve feelings of jealously that partners may have. All of these factors strongly work to create or destroy celebrity relationships," says Houran. The filming of sex scenes causes "worries about fidelity"—and in the case of Aniston and Pitt, for instance, there was indeed cause for worry while Pitt was filming *Mr. and Mrs. Smith*.

If two stars are of equal popularity, "unconscious feelings of competition and resentment" can arise in their relationship, according to Houran. He goes on to say that "sex and money are the two leading causes of relationship breakups for the general public as they are tied to control and power. But for celebrities, they offer freedom to pursue impulsive fantasies or other indulgences that can undermine a relationship."

Addicted to Love

There is something else that can contribute to celebrities making relationship mistakes. And it's something we can all relate to: a passion for what they do, a love of their craft.

The passion of falling in love and the passion of taking on a new film role trigger the brain in the same way. (And so too, interestingly enough, does substance abuse and other addictive behaviors.) So, Robert Palmer wasn't too far off when he sang "Addicted to Love."

It works like this: When the human brain experiences this kind of pleasure, the levels of the hormones dopamine, adrenaline, and serotonin increase. When those hormones kick in, you can't think logically. That's why you are better off waiting until that first flush has waned to assess your partner in a realistic way rather than in an impulsive way.

When those chemicals are raging and you get dumped, you feel incredibly devastated. It's like being addicted to drugs and then suddenly being forced to go cold turkey. But a celebrity doesn't have to stay off her drug for too long: She just needs to show up at the Beverly Wilshire Hotel and I'm sure some young Hollywood hunk licking *his* wounds will be there. If not, she can call her publicist and arrange an introduction . . . done! Stars also have the opportunity to be cast in a new film or involved in a new project—something new to get those passion triggers in their brains flowing again. While the rest of us have only Ben and Jerry to comfort us.

CHAPTER ELEVEN

Pumps, Humps, and Baby Bumps

All women do have a different sense of sexuality, or sense of fun, or sense of like what's sexy or cool or tough . . .

Angelina Jolie, in *Esquire* magazine, February 2000

I was on the *Tyra Banks Show*. Maybe you saw it. I was there to tell Tyra and her audience how to "Decode Their Man." Decoding men is a pastime of mine; I started young. When I was in the fifth grade, I knew Mark Dexter liked me when he poured juice on the floor and told everyone that I peed. It wasn't until that summer when I hit him across the face with a hockey stick that I abruptly ended our budding romance. He asked me out again in high school, so I knew I was right on target.

But decoding men isn't all that hard if you think about it—what's there to decode? Men are simple creatures, and I didn't need all of the research that I brought with me to the Tyra show to prove my point. I just wanted to share what the science had to say with an audience who, as it turned out, was looking for uncomplicated answers. Men are indeed uncomplicated, so they weren't far off. I reminded them of things they already knew and then shed some light on a few mysteries. Tyra never did a follow-up, a part two—"How to Decode Your Woman"—because nobody has ever been able to. Women are hard to decode, and celebrity women are virtually impossible.

Famous men, however, are just as straightforward as regular men, so their image makers don't face the same challenges as those of female stars. Male celebrities don't make sex tapes, or if they do, we just don't care. That's because men having sex isn't scandalous. Scantily clad men are not provocative—not to straight women, anyway. Even David Beckham's oversize (some say doctored) package in that Armani underwear ad only enhanced his image. He didn't seem slutty, sad, pathetic, or objectified. In fact perhaps the main reason the Beckham ads were so noticeable was simply the rarity of seeing a male celebrity in such an overtly sexual pose. If it had been a sexy female celebrity reclining in her underwear—maybe with, gasp, padding to highlight her cleavage—the ads would have created barely a ripple.

This may be why people went nuts when the unconventional Maggie Gyllenhaal posed in teddies and garters for Agent Provocateur. It wasn't because she was so provocative, but because she *wasn't.* She was criticized for being unsexy, too old, and an acquired taste, as opposed to previous models for the lingerie line such as Kate Moss and burlesque star Dita von Teese, who were universally accepted as sexy, young, or voluptuous. Gyllenhaal is nonthreatening like a regular woman and doesn't look like a supermodel or a Hollywood starlet; she looked the way a plain Jane would look in handcuffs and a garter.

The ads were designed to appeal to the thirtysomething married woman, not sixteen-year-olds who are searching for a sexual identity. Most teen girls have no idea who Gyllenhaal is, unlike, say, Jessica Simpson or Fergie, two celebrities who also appear in highly sexualized ads. I for one was glad to see Gyllenhaal breaking the stereotype of the lingerie model and representing ordinary women's sexuality, because sexy ads featuring young girls' celebrity idols drive me bonkers. My good friend's thirteen-year-old daughter Caitlin has them plastered all over her bedroom wall. I don't get it, and it does concern me that she could be so heavily influenced by ads for products suitable not for young teens but for adults.

Hypersex Is the New Cybersex

Female athletes who, at their core, are better images of female achievement and beauty for younger teens to admire than, say, Nicole Richie, are overwhelmingly shown in the same highly sexualized poses reserved for a Mark Jacobs ad. Magazines don't make the distinction; it's not their job. We as parents or simply as consumers have to do it.

Not That Innocent

I have never told anybody this before, but I have an odd habit. Before I sit down to read a fashion magazine, I have to rip out all of the ads so that I can focus on the content. It's an annoying sound on airplanes and subways and even more annoying when I do it on the bike at the gym . . . *rip, rip, rip*. But the ads take away my enjoyment of salivating over the latest Chloé bag and then seething over its price tag. I want to lose myself in an article about how to get eye makeup and a blowout to last longer without being disturbed by those obnoxious perfume ads that stink up my day. Yet young Caitlin can't get enough, despite the fact that the ads are way too sexy and highly inappropriate for her age group. This is indeed a problem, and here's why . . .

Cognitive and emotional consequences. Highly sexualized images of "perfect" women undermine a girl's comfort with her own body. Since we live in a world where body image and self-image are intertwined, this leads to emotional and self-image problems. (As a side note, images of sexed-up, young female celebrities might not be the worst offender in undermining girls' body image. That dubious distinction goes to ads that focus exclusively on one body part, as though women are chicken: Here's a perfect wing, thigh, or breast . . .)

Mental and physical health. Kimberly Lawrence Kol, Psy.D., clinical psychologist and eating disorder specialist, links exposure to over-sexualized images with three of the most common mental health problems diagnosed in girls: eating disorders and depression, which leads to the third, low self-esteem.

Sexual development. In many teenage circles the boys have all the power. They decide who is popular and who is not based on who they are attracted to and who they aren't. These are important years for sexual-identity development, and if being sexy and looking sexy is what they value, there's trouble brewing. Images of sexy and provocative young female celebrities have the potential to reinforce that value system.

Parents are even more concerned about preteen, or "tween," girls. They worry that the sexy images they see of celebrities affect their development, and psychologists agree that the sexualization of young girls is a key area in which parents need to be diligent. In response to public concern, the American Psychological Association (APA) put together a task force of renowned psychologists to address the issue. They defined sexualization as the state where

"Such ads often take a star popular with teens and preteens and present her in highly sexualized poses."

—AMERICAN PSYCHOLOGICAL ASSOCIATION

a person is portrayed as merely a sexual object, where the person's value comes only from his or her sexual appeal or behavior.

In their report they identified plenty of evidence of the sexualization of young girls, including such things as thong underwear with the words EYE CANDY printed on them being marketed to girls as young as seven. They cite advertising campaigns that parents have a right to be offended by because of the negative impact they may have on young girls: the ads that Christina Aguilera did for Skechers where she played two roles, one naughty and one nice; the Abercrombie and Fitch catalogue; and the Paris Hilton Carl's Jr. hamburger ads. "Such ads often take a star popular with teens and preteens and present her in highly sexualized poses," reads the APA's report. "Some explicitly play up innocence as sexy, as in one of the Skechers 'naughty and nice' ads that featured Aguilera dressed as a schoolgirl in pigtails, with her shirt unbuttoned, licking a lollipop."

The APA's conclusion? They say that "the proliferation of sexualized images of girls and young women in advertising, merchandising, and media is harming girls' self-image and healthy development."

Some moms may feel that their daughter's choice of sexy adult fashions is merely "self-expression." One mom told me that "clothing is the healthiest way for my daughter to express herself." The APA disagrees: "It is of concern when girls at increasingly younger ages are invited to try on and wear teen clothes designed to highlight female sexuality." What those clothes do is validate young girls as sexual beings. A word for you parents out there: Your daughter is so much more. Her self-worth should be based on more than her looks, and you need to show her that her value lies in who she is, her integrity, her compassion, her character, and her optimism for her own future. It should not be based on the size of her breasts. The tween ages are incredibly important years; this is when identity development happens, according to many theories, so you as a parent need to be vigilant. You may not have control over what is presented in the media, but you certainly do have control over what your child wears and reads.

Dr. Lawrence Kol says, "Parents need to actively help their kid understand what they're consuming." She suggests parents have a conversation with their children regarding images such as those the APA refers to, — ads in magazines that are excessively provocative—and say, "I won't buy that fashion magazine for you, but if you do read one, pay attention to how badly you feel about yourself after you read it."

TMI

In addition to the messages sexy celebrity advertisements send to young girls, parents also worry about the overall hypersexual

Consume media with care. Kimberly Lawrence Kol, Psy.D., reminds parents to help their children learn how to consume the media. "If I am a kid and I don't know that I'm being sold things 100 percent of the time, then I'm gonna buy into it unless I have a parent who says, 'Hey you're being sold something.'" Advertising and marketing are sophisticated, powerful, and abundant. Since kids are most vulnerable, you need to help them navigate the media.

images of their daughters' favorite celebrities. This is a new phenomenon. I don't think my parents were concerned because Marcia Brady wore a skirt above her knee. After all, the rest of the dress fit her like a nun's habit, covering her arms down to the knuckles and her neck and chest up to the chin.

Since time immemorial little girls have imitated grown-ups—maybe not so bad when it meant putting on Mom's shoes, accessorizing with a feather boa and some smudged lipstick, and clomping all around the house. But what if it means emulating a barely clad, gyrating and grinding, moaning and ahhing, possibly pantiless starlet? Kids love their favorite stars with a kind of utter and total devotion that it's easy to forget when you're an adult. In 2007 I was on a show called the *Morning Show with Mike and Juliet* for my local Fox Channel with a woman named Kathleen Deveny, a *Newsweek* writer whose six-year-old daughter "loves, loves, *loves*" Lindsay Lohan. In a piece she wrote for the magazine, she asked a question on many parents' minds: "Are we raising a generation of 'prosti-tots'?" When a picture of Lohan taking pole-dancing classes appeared in the newspaper, she was at a loss for words when her daughter said, "That's Lindsay Lohan. . . . What's she doing?" A poll conducted by *Newsweek* around the same time found that 77 percent of Americans believed that Britney Spears, Paris Hilton, and Lindsay Lohan had too much influence on young girls.

Seventy-seven percent of Americans believed that Britney Spears, Paris Hilton, and Lindsay Lohan had too much influence on young girls.

In the past we didn't have such scantily clad lead characters on TV shows, getting younger and younger all the time. We didn't have pubescent ex-Mousketeers singing about what they'd like to have done to them by their man, starlets with a personal style combining schoolgirl and pro, and music video choreography straight out of a lap-dancing club. We didn't have *Bratz*.

Just one generation ago children grew up watching *Little House on the Prairie* and the *Mary Tyler Moore Show*. Mary was certainly attractive, but not gorgeous and sexy in the way that she would be expected to be now. With the advent of hits such as *Buffy, the Vampire Slayer*, *Friends*, and *Dawson's Creek*, and all of that Jennifer beauty (Aniston, Lopez, Garner, Love Hewitt, and Connelly), TV started to look like much more of a fashion show. Teen and tween hits such as *The O.C.*, *Gossip Girl*, and *The Hills* all look pretty much like the producers swung by a top modeling agency and scooped up whichever super-sexy young things happened to be hanging around the reception desk waiting to be sent on a go-see.

If you are concerned that your daughter may be finding out too much about sex at too young an age and you want to try and stop that train from barreling down on her, well then, good luck. That would mean cutting her off from the deluge of celebrity personal sexual information in magazines and on the Internet and from TV completely. We are in the age of TMI as SOP (Too Much Information as Standard Operating Procedure).

Kids are watching a record number of hours of television; study after study reveals that they spend more time with the TV than any other medium and TV has been referred to as the "super-peer." In 2004, researchers at Michigan State University had a group of fifth to eighth graders log how much TV they watched regularly (specifically shows aimed at them) and how much sexual content they saw. They found that 60 percent of the programs watched by this group of eleven- to fifteen-year-olds had high sexual content, ranging from passionate kissing to intercourse.

Another study found that sometimes TV shows with sexual content open the lines of communication, but to be helpful, they have to be age appropriate. That study, published in the journal *Pediatrics*, showed that after an episode of *Friends* that addressed the issue of condom failure, the twelve- to seventeen-year-old children in the study had almost a 20 percent increase in condom awareness and were more likely to ask their parents about the efficacy of condoms. Some parents embraced it as a chance to open a discussion; for others it elicited fear that now their kids

Put your preconceptions aside. This is a whole different generation, so if you want to talk to a young person about sex in any real way, you have to put aside all that you knew before. These kids are growing up being told by the media that oral sex is not sex, and they have had sexual images thrown at them since they could walk. So drop any old-fashioned ideas about sex education you might have and follow these steps: (1) Start early. (2) Use the real names for body parts. (3) Bring up the topic—don't wait for them to. (4) Talk beyond "birds and bees," meaning let them know that real sexual relationships are about love, caring, and emotion. The same applies for opening up a discussion about gay men and lesbians, if your child has questions.

would want to go have sex. I have great news for those parents: Studies show that the opposite is true. If a child is able to talk to their parents about sex—at any age—and if they are armed with knowledge, they are less likely to have intercourse as a young teenager.

Perhaps Jamie Lynn Spears missed that conversation with her mother. When the sixteen-year-old star of Nickelodeon's *Zoey 101* announced that she was pregnant in 2007, her face was plastered across the cover of every celebrity weekly. Then when she announced that she would accept $1 million from a tabloid for the exclusive photos of her baby, she was talked about incessantly everywhere. This was not an issue exclusively affecting twelve- to seventeen-year-olds, because Jamie Lynn's fans were not just teens. They were seven, they were ten—they were young, young children.

So now you have to be prepared to have a conversation with your eight-year-old about sex? Then, do you have to explain that becoming pregnant at sixteen doesn't win everyone a million dollar consolation prize? Some said it was an opportunity to have the conversation with your kids; others said it wasn't age appropriate and blamed Nickelodeon for not having a clause in her contract to preserve her churchgoing schoolgirl image.

I, and many of my talking head cohorts of course, were called to discuss this on *Showbiz Tonight* and other entertainment news shows. That wasn't surprising, because it was indeed entertainment news. What was surprising was that I was also called in to

When in doubt, Dr. Judy it! One of the women I admire most is clinical psychologist Judy Kuriansky, Ph.D., who gives great advice for having the sex/pregnancy talk with your kids, especially after a beloved young starlet comes out and says, "Hey, I'm pregnant." Kuriansky says that parents are afraid of this conversation, because either they don't know what to say or their own background makes them feel like a hypocrite. Once on CNN she said, "Don't take the ostrich approach. Kids will be talking about this in school and with other kids, so ask them what they have heard and what they already know." Let's face it, you don't want your twelve-year-old getting sex advice from other twelve-year-olds, right?

discuss the young Spears girl on Fox News's *Your World with Neil Cavuto*. Cavuto did ask me sarcastically why the Western world had been brought to its knees by this non-news story. (Oh, if only he had a national television show to air his viewpoint.) But it was news, and here's what the news bulletin should have been: "This just in, Social Learning Theory at work, you may need to *actually* lock up your daughters."

Social Learning Theory is one of the most significant ideas to come along in the last forty years. Its leading proponent, psychologist Albert Bandura, proved that we learn by observing the actions of others. In one of his most well-known experiments, different groups of children were given a "Bobo Doll," an inflatable toy a few feet tall that bounces right back up if you hit it. They'd never seen the toy before and didn't know how to use it. Some groups of children were shown an adult hitting the doll violently. And just as predicted, when those children took their turn with poor Bobo, they were far more likely than the other kids to hit him violently. The children who treated Bobo violently were behaving in a way they felt was expected of them; they were behaving the way an adult had showed them they should behave.

Social Learning Theory applies not only to violent behavior. The next time you find your ten-year-old admiring pictures of a celebrity that you deem a deplorable and harmful role model, think of that Bobo Doll and what he signifies: Kids model their behavior on adults. This is another good reason why us adults have to remember that we need to keep a watchful eye on the media and entertainment young children are consuming—and be mindful of our own behavior, too.

Fight early hypersexualization. It's not all in your head: There *is* a difference between celebrity and media images girls see now and what you were exposed to as a child. Highly sexualized images of younger and younger women are becoming the norm. It's hard to resist the desperate pleas of a fashion-conscious tween begging for the latest outfits or for makeup, jewelry, shoes, handbags—oh, the list goes on and on of what they "need, like, really, really need, Mom"—but don't forget that you're the one with the pocketbook. You're the one who has the final say on whether an outfit is age appropriate. You're also the one who has the final say on what your children watch and read. You can express your feelings with your wallet—by *closing* it and not buying products that are marketed inappropriately. Also, don't forget, communication—talking honestly to your kids about what they see and hear—is also very important.

Entertaining Gays

The celebrity influence on attitudes to sex extends beyond the link with the hypersexualizing of girls today. The TV shows, movies, music, and celebrity news we absorb help inform all our views—adults included—on the whole range of human sexuality.

Actors, musicians, entertainers, artists, and writers have long pushed the boundaries of what we consider tasteful, moral, and acceptable. They both ride and help swell the tides of social change—and that includes our changing attitudes toward sex.

One of the clearest examples I can think of is in relation to views on homosexuality.

There's a famous scene in Neil Simon's *Brighton Beach Memoirs* where Aunt Blanche whispers the word *cancer*, as though if you say it out loud it may hear you; as though the word is verboten, not something you say aloud in polite company. People used to feel that way with the word *gay*. Some still do, but their numbers are shrinking. Words such as *gay*, *homosexual*, and *lesbian* are now heard all the time in films, on TV, and in the world of celebrity culture. This is a good thing. Words that used to shock many and anger some have become no big deal.

The best way to overcome any prejudice, be it religious, ethnic, or sexual, is to have personal experience with someone who is of a different religion, culture, or sexuality. In the absence of someone in your day-to-day life, you have celebrities. Psychologists call this kind of connection "media contact," and when it comes to breaking down prejudice it can be as effective as real, personal contact. Someone who doesn't know any lesbians has Rosie O'Donnell, Melissa Etheridge, and

Someone who doesn't know any lesbians has Rosie O'Donnell, Melissa Etheridge, and Ellen DeGeneres as great examples.

Ellen DeGeneres as great examples. Research shows that media contact does help bridge the gap between gay and straight people, reducing the likelihood of homophobia.

Will and Grace used humor to break the ice with viewers who might have never directly experienced someone who was gay. If it weren't for shows such as *Will and Grace* that included gay characters who were more than just flamboyant queens sashaying their way through the sale racks at Barney's, perhaps we wouldn't have had the success of shows such as *Queer Eye for the Straight Guy, Six Feet Under, Brothers and Sisters,* and myriad other TV shows featuring "out" characters.

It's a two-way street. The fact that stars as big as DeGeneres and O'Donnell have publicly donned the moniker *lesbian* not only softens public attitudes, it also *reflects* how public attitudes are softening. Jean Twenge of the University of San Diego and her colleagues say that this generation is much more tolerant of what used to be called an "alternative lifestyle." A study out of the Chicago School of Professional Psychology confirms this idea, saying, "Culture and society at large have become more accepting of the gay community, . . . The number of openly gay youths is unprecedented, and they are coming out at younger ages than ever before."

When Dick Cheney's daughter Mary came out to her high-profile neo-con dad, it marked a turning point. In the past, lesbianism was barely recognized by society, but when it was, "it was considered a perversion and generally regarded as synonymous with depravity," says Martha Gever in her book *Entertaining Lesbians: Celebrity, Sexuality and Self Invention.* That meant that lesbian women in the public eye were hardly about to admit to their sexual preference. The situation changed during the late twentieth century when a phenomenon was born that Gever has termed "lesbian celebrity."

We have become accustomed in recent years to female celebrities coming out, but for male stars it's one thing to portray a gay character and quite another to reveal they are homosexual in real life. Rumors have circulated for years about certain film actors and their sexual proclivities, and to a degree it is still taboo for males to be out in Hollywood. But this has more to do with sexism than it does with celebrity.

Rumors have circulated for years about certain film actors and their sexual proclivities, and to a degree it is still taboo for males to be out in Hollywood.

For most of human history, female sexuality was a non-issue, according to Colin Spencer, who wrote *Homosexuality: A History*. The reason? In a male-dominated society, nobody cared what women did. Lesbianism mostly went under the radar, partly from a belief that no penetration equaled no sex, but mostly due to the "Who cares what women do?" thing. This may be why it's okay for women to come out in Hollywood but not okay for men: Because Hollywood is still extremely male dominated.

Just look at any epic film made over the last ten years. Chances are, anywhere from five to eight of the lead characters are male, whereas only one or two are female. The *Oceans Eleven* series is a great example. (Not that I'm implying

George Clooney, Brad Pitt, or Matt Damon are gay, although even if they were, I would drool over any one of them still.) Need more proof of the gender inequality in Hollywood? In 2007, Reese Witherspoon was crowned the highest-paid actress in Hollywood, garnering $15 million to $20 million per film. Which sounds great, until you learn that Mel Gibson and Tom Cruise were usually making about $30 million a film . . . oh, plus a share of the movie's box office profits, according to Michelle Grabicki of the *Hollywood Reporter*. Johnny Depp earned $92 million in one year, mostly thanks to the *Pirates of the Caribbean* franchise. You're probably saying, "What about Oprah? Her salary has been reported at $260 million a year." But remember, we are talking about actors who rely solely on their acting for their income. Not folks who have their own network and magazines.

Bump Watch America

The late twentieth century was a time of sexual revolutions for women. You might immediately think of the pill, *Roe v. Wade*, the freedom to shack up without getting married—but on newsstands and TV screens all across the country another, perhaps quieter but no less significant, revolution in female sexuality has been unfolding. Let me introduce you to a little phenomenon that has been referred to as "bump watch."

Nowhere in our culture has nudity become more passé than in the world of celebrity, especially in the past ten years or so. If you haven't posed nude for *Playboy*, a tabloid hasn't caught you without undergarments, or you have not been photographed at a red carpet event without at least one exposed nipple, then you aren't anyone—or anyone who matters. Even celebrity unborn children get their moment of fame. It has become a celebrity mom-to-be prerequisite to be photographed full-frontal pregnancy and to sell to the highest bidder the exclusive photos of the as-yet-unborn fetus the minute air hits its lungs.

But let me rewind for a moment. The idea of women baring their flesh on the screen was once so scandalous that Barbara Eden's exposed navel in the mid-1960s in *I Dream of Jeannie* shocked many viewers. TV and film producers were coy not only about female sexuality but also its frequent consequence: pregnancy. So imagine the ruckus in 1953 when Lucille Ball forced CBS executives to write her real-life pregnancy into the second season of her show. So sensitive was the topic that "this television first was monitored carefully by a trio of clergy who oversaw each script," according to an article by the Museum of Broadcast Communication. The writers had to substitute the word *expectant* for the earthier *pregnant*. But as it turns out, the public was ready for it. The seven-episode arc was as riveting as it was controversial, earning the show record-setting ratings, with "more viewers tuning in to witness the fictional Lucy Ricardo give birth than had seen Eisenhower's inauguration."

It has become a celebrity mom-to-be prerequisite to be photographed full-frontal pregnancy.

Cut to November 2007 when *Marie Claire* published some unremarkable and non-newsworthy photographs of a very naked and very pregnant Christina Aguilera . . . ho hum, it was *so* 1991. That's when the now infamous Annie Leibovitz photograph of a pregnant Demi Moore graced the cover of *Vanity Fair*, stirring up a great deal of trouble. Many stores refused to sell the magazine, and many of the ones that did kept it in a brown paper bag as if it were a copy of *Jugs*. Leibovitz's intention was to portray the star with an antiglitz, antiglamour, anti-Hollywood image—as a real woman, strong and powerful. Ironic when you consider how Hollywood it has become to be photographed pregnant.

Fortunately nudity in the everyday world still has shock value and is considered objectionable. Humor columnist Mike Nichols (not the director) describes it this way: "Take off all your clothes and walk down the street waving a machete and firing an Uzi, and terrified citizens will phone the police and report, 'There's a naked person outside!'" Yet for a celebrity, being photographed naked and/or pregnant is de rigueur, as if their datebook reads: *breakfast with director, script read-through, be photographed with exposed belly, arrive at red carpet by 6.*

Our growing acceptance of celebrity pregnancy is mirrored by pregnant stars gradually exposing more and more of themselves, both emotionally and physically. Since the notorious Moore picture, Denise Richards, Gwen Stefani, Gwyneth Paltrow, Courtney Cox, and Reese Witherspoon have all been photographed proudly with their bellies exposed to the camera instead of hiding them behind a tote or newspaper. Some were wearing cute belly shirts, others high-end maternity wear, but none of them were hiding the fact that she was with child.

While the naked, styled, professionally coiffed, and made-up pregnant star sprawled across the pages of a magazine has clearly made a conscious choice to appear that way, you may be surprised to learn that even the casual paparazzi shots of celebrities blooming with the glow of pregnancy are sometimes no accident either. Allison Corneau of Usmagazine.com explains that some of it is very calculated. "When a celeb like Sarah Jessica Parker is photographed everywhere—pregnant or otherwise—one has to remember that SJP is pushing her clothing line, Bitten, and any other projects she is working on. Just as ubiquitous is Jennifer Lopez, who wants you to buy her fragrances, her music, and her Sweetface clothing. There are indeed lots of avenues for stars to be exposed and they realize that each time they are spotted, it could signify financial gain."

You may be offended by the incessant "bump watch" of celebrity weeklies as they tail Angelina Jolie or Jennifer Lopez to the grocery store. On the other hand, you may feel that women are empowered by their effervescent glow when they are with child and should be celebrated. Either way, somewhere in the early part of the decade it became a national pastime to look for the baby bump of your favorite star; it's a sort of the *Where's Waldo?* approach to motherhood.

The iconic status of celebrity pregnancy and the eagerness of some stars to publicize the result of a night of passion feed into a larger cultural debate over what it means to be a mother in America. Perceptions of motherhood are in a state of flux. According to the U.S. Census Bureau, the number of stay-at-home moms in 2005 was 5.6 million, up from 4.4 million a decade earlier. The Census also reported that 55 percent of mothers with infant children continued to stay in the labor force, down from a record high of 59 percent in 1998. The number of single mothers living with children younger than eighteen was 10.4 million, up from 3.4 million in 1970. With a little over 80.5 million mothers nationwide, what is motherhood in America? That definition is really up to you.

In her article "The Mixed Messages of Motherhood," Joy Rice of the University of Wisconsin says, "Although *motherhood* is shared by many women, it is difficult to make accurate generalizations about their experiences. In addition, no woman resembles the romanticized notion of the ideal mother." We have the benefit of endless information about prenatal care, abstinence, birth control, and pregnancy, and we have a level of control over our educations, careers, and finances that women of earlier generations could only fantasize about. That all gives us the power to define motherhood any way we want to, as individuals. It is unfathomable to us today that in 1905 Theodore Roosevelt gave a speech in which he said ". . . the primary duty of the husband is to be the home-maker, the breadwinner for his wife and children, and . . . the primary duty of the woman is to be the helpmate, the housewife, and mother." Yet we have also outgrown pioneering feminist Betty Friedan's idea that a housewife is a "parasite."

Celebrities break barriers publicly that we have already broken privately.

At the Vanguard

Celebrity culture not only influences our culture, it reflects our culture. That means that while we need to be mindful of the sexualized images young girls see and need to monitor who their celebrity idols are, we need to be just as focused on all the other aspects of girls' lives. Celebrities are riding the crest of the wave of change, so when we are troubled by what we see in the media, it means we need to look deeper for the causes.

Fortunately, there are some signs coming from the world of entertainment and celebrity that we should celebrate—signs of changing attitudes that indicate more freedom to express our individual sexuality. Gay men and women are increasingly visible and accepted on our TV and movie screens, just as they are in daily life. And perceptions are changing of mothers, too.

What we see in the images of pregnant celebrities are women expressing an emerging identity in which motherhood no longer means giving up your sexuality, in which women can combine family and career, and in which choosing to have children doesn't mean losing your place in the world. Pregnancy and the right to feel and look sexy are no longer mutually exclusive. Celebrities break barriers publicly that we have already broken privately. They take to the public stage that which is already in motion in the American vanguard; they are the town criers of the authentic experience of our own lives. We do it, they shout about it.

In Conclusion

I used to work as an entertainment reporter for a radio prep service that provided content for radio shows around the country that did not have access to big-name celebrities. I would go to press junkets for films or round-table interviews in hotel rooms, where I and five or six other journalists would literally sit at a round table taking turns asking the celebrity questions. Then I'd file entertainment news reports and sound bites from the interview that radio stations could use on air. At the same time, I was also writing for a magazine, again covering entertainment news but for a much hipper, younger audience. So in one week I would interview an actor who had been around for a long time and a new young upstart who was said to be the next big thing.

It gave me firsthand experience with the Machine. One week I was interviewing David Ogden Stiers, who played Charles Emerson Winchester III on the hit TV show *M*A*S*H,* and comedienne Janeane Garofalo, whose career was on the rise at the time. I called to set up a time to speak with Stiers and was surprised when he answered the phone, rather than an assistant. After all, he was an established performer, a Julliard-trained actor mentored by the great John Houseman. He had starred in many highly acclaimed theater, TV, and film productions, including several Woody Allen films and my favorite guilty pleasure, *Better Off Dead.* "How's next Thursday at 4:00 p.m.?" he said and then gave me the address.

Flush with success, I felt undaunted as I dialed the number for Garofalo, but I was to have quite a different experience. She did not answer the phone, and the assistant who did asked me to fax my request, on letterhead, to their office and they would get back to me. After three days and my deadline drawing near, I phoned and was again asked to fax a request. When I explained that I had done so already, the assistant asked what the interview was for, what questions I would be asking, and how much time I would need with Garofalo. "Good news," I thought. "She sounds interested."

I waited three more days for a phone call to set up a time. When that call did not come, I phoned one last time. I just needed to know either way. If it was a "no," that would be fine with me—just tell me, I'm a big girl. On this occasion I was asked to send over articles I had written on other celebrities, for Garofalo to review. I did that and never heard back. My guess is that none of the information I sent made it to the comedienne's desk. I'm not sure anything I sent even made it past the assistant's desk, but so goes the Machine.

The next day when I arrived for my interview with Stiers, I told him of the contrast between setting up an interview with him, a well-respected actor from the old school, and someone from the new school of celebrity. He shared his reflections on acting great Henry Fonda, who had a humbler attitude than the majority of stars do today.

Stiers was doing a play with "Fonda" (which is what the cast all called him), who would drive himself to work every day in a beat-up old Volvo. You could tell Fonda wasn't the best driver: His car had doors that didn't match, hubcaps missing, and a few dings here and there that he'd decided weren't worth fixing, as the car would just get dinged-up again. Yet he didn't ask for a limousine, there were no assistants running around getting him water—he was just another actor at the theater doing his job. The business has certainly changed when someone like Henry Fonda, who had earned the right to be a real diva (or I guess divo in this case), was just another poor schlub going to work every day. Yet when J Lo goes on tour, she stipulates that in every town she plays her dressing room must be white and stocked with white flowers, white tables, white drapes, white couches, white sheets, and tuberose, fig, and heliotrope–scented Diptyque candles (which are, I'm guessing, white).

This makes me think of the studies cited in this book that show a rise in narcissism in young people, the notion that narcissism is inherent in many people who seek the spotlight, and the acquired situational narcissism celebrities are at risk of developing when they hit the big time. Perhaps it is this personality trait that makes celebrities feel they should be treated differently from everyone else and that this sets them apart from the rest of us, even early on in their careers.

Or perhaps it is the amount of money stars are worth now. I'm not just talking about the celebrities' fortunes but also the many livelihoods that depend upon them. Take Britney Spears: According to Conde Nast's Portfolio.com, BritBrit has made Elizabeth Arden over $100 million with her perfume sales, her albums have made Jive records over $400 million, and her concert tours have grossed nearly $150 million. Even now she commands $250,000 to $400,000 for an appearance fee, meaning "Britney, can you stop by my club?" will cost you a bundle. The magazine industry has benefited as well with celeb gossip magazines posting staggering sales numbers when Britney graces the cover. Not to mention all the paparazzi who sell the exclusive shots to the magazines for thousands of dollars. And there are other, less obvious, profits—or expenses, depending on which side of the ledger you're on. On one of the many occasions when Spears and Kevin Federline were in court to fight for custody of their kids, the LA County Sheriff's Department "billed the court $2286.10 to cover the cost of extra security." The Spears-generated economy benefited not only the security firm but a host of legal staff, too.

The incredible earning power of stars and the microeconomies they support have contributed to their unique place in society. Perhaps celebrities are afforded a status above mortal human beings because they are such valuable commodities.

But why do we care so much about these often-narcissistic commodities? They have acting and singing talents, charm and charisma, and good looks. We have all been swept up in a beautiful song or found meaning and comfort in an actor's performance and suddenly felt a strong connection with them. Yet none of these forces, as powerful as they are, fully explain the spell that celebrity has on our culture at this time.

Some of us like the one-sidedness of our relationship with a celebrity—it's much easier than complex and difficult relationships in the real world. Some of us get vicarious enjoyment out of following the lives of stars, including a little bit of schadenfreude when things go wrong in their lives. As much as we hate to admit it, seeing the misfortunes of stars can make us feel better about ourselves. A small number of people, for whom celebrity worship is a problem that has taken over their lives, have issues with neuroticism or narcissism.

I think our widespread fascination with celebrity has little to do with the talents and charisma of the celebrities themselves but is more about our need to form bonds and social connections with others. You can go to Japan, meet a complete stranger, and say

"Angelina Jolie" and there, you have bonded. Same goes for more familiar scenarios such as going to a party with people you barely know, or chatting with your coworkers in the break room.

When we tell others a story we have read in a celebrity magazine—or better yet, recount our own celebrity sighting—it enhances our social relationships with them. With busy and often socially disconnected lives, celebrity worship may be one way to strengthen the social bonds that make us human. And perhaps *that* is what we are all really craving.

Index

Index

Acknowledgments

A special thank you to Maura Teitelbaum whose unwavering support and friendship I would be lost without. I am indebted to everyone who shared their stories with me on my radio show, or generously gave of their time to offer their expert opinions, specifically:

The Celebrities... Marcia Gay Harden, Kevin Federline, Edwin McCain, Mike Farrell, Peter Criss, Stephen Collins, Rita Cosby, Fran Drescher, Leven Rambin, Constantine Maroulis, and Ereka Vetrini.

The Experts... Jarett Weiselman, Dr. Kimberly Kol, Mark Turner, Robert Attermann, Barbara Skydel, Susan Blond, Jennifer Nuccio, Dr. Jason Plaks, Dr. Peter Scales, Jeannine Hill Fletcher, Th.D, Darryll Brooks, David Levine, Leo Braudy, Christina Beck, James Houran, Ph.D., Stacy Schneider Esq., Olivia Harris, Dr. Diane Madfes, and Allison Corneau.

My Globe Pequot/skirt! Books Family... Scott Watrous, Gary Krebs, Michelle Lewy, Inger Forland, editors Vanessa Mickan-Gramazio, Mary Norris, and Imee Curiel, and publicist Justin "Raul" Loeber.

My Radio Family... Kirk Stirland, Anthony Michaels, and Chad Bowar.

My Actual Family... my parents Sandi and Bob Durell and my wonderful saintly husband, Sean Lee.

About the Author

COOPER LAWRENCE is one of the foremost authorities on celebrity culture and fame. She can be seen as the fame expert on VH1's *Confessions of a Teen Idol.* She holds a master's degree in psychology from Fordham University and is currently finishing her doctorate.

Cooper hosts the nationally syndicated talk radio show, *The Cooper Lawrence Show* from Dial Global. Her show combines entertainment, pop culture, comedy, and celebrity all flavored with Cooper's unique brand of storytelling. To find a station that carries the show near you or to listen live online, go to www.cooperlawrenceshow.com.

Cooper can be seen regularly on CNN Headline News's *Showbiz Tonight* and *The Tyra Banks Show* as well as other shows including, *The Today Show, The Early Show, The O'Reilly Factor, Your World with Neil Cavuto, Hannity & Colmes, Fox & Friends, The Insider,* and on *E! Entertainment Television.* She has been featured in print for the *New York Post, New York Daily News, Chicago Tribune, IN STYLE, SELF, Parenting, Cosmopolitan, Family Circle, OK! Magazine, US Weekly, Life & Style, Star Magazine, In Touch Weekly, The Huffington Post,* and *CosmoGIRL!*

Previous books include *The Cult of Perfection: Making Peace with Your Inner Overachiever*; *The Fixer Upper Man*: *Turn Mr. Maybe Into Mr. Right; Been There, Done That, Kept the Jewelry;* and *CosmoGIRL's All About Guys*.

A portion of the sales of *The Cult Of Celebrity* will go to Angel On A Leash, a charity of the Westminster Kennel Club that champions working with therapy dogs in health care facilities, schools, rehabilitation, hospice, extended care, correctional facilities, and crisis intervention. For more information or to support Angel On A Leash, please go to www.angelonaleash.org.

Cooper lives with her husband, Sean, in New York City.